The Miso Cookbook

87 Umami-Rich Recipes Using Japan's Incredible Probiotic Superfood

MISA ENOMOTO

TUTTLE Publishing
Tokyo | Rutland, Vermont | Singapore

CONTENTS

INTRODUCTION
An Easy Way to Enhance Every Meal! 4

All About Homemade Overnight Miso

What Makes Homemade Miso so Delicious? 6
The Health Benefits of Homemade Miso 7
Nutrients in Homemade Miso 8
How to Make Homemade Miso Overnight 10
Homemade Miso Made with Other Beans 14
Homemade Miso Q & A 16

Homemade Miso Makes the Best Miso Soup!

Onion and Carrot Miso Soup with Ginger 18
Leek and Tofu Miso Soup 19
Sake Lees Soup with Salmon and Taro 20
Pork and Root Vegetable Miso Soup 21
Chicken and Cabbage Miso Soup 22
Miso Soup with Yam and Seaweed 22
Spicy Miso Soup with Pea Shoots 23
Miso Soup with Komatsuna and Egg 23
Miso Soup with Turnip and Baby Sardines 24
Cabbage and Shrimp Miso Soup 24
Miso Soup with Asparagus and Onion 25
Green Pepper and Pork Miso Soup 25
Miso Soup with Eggplant 26
Mushroom Miso Soup 26
Yam and Okra Miso Soup 27
Miso Soup with Cauliflower 27
Tomato and Bacon Soup 28
Kabocha Miso Soup 28
Potato and Corn Miso Soup with Soy Milk 29

Instant Miso Soup

Wakame and Fu Instant Miso Soup 30
Nori and Sesame Instant Miso Soup 31
Kombu and Umeboshi Instant Miso Soup 31
Mitsuba and Ginger Instant Miso Soup 32
Myoga and Shiso Instant Miso Soup 32

Simply Seasoned Snacks

Miso Butter Toast 34
Miso Rice Balls with Shiso 35
Miso Grilled Turnip 35
Miso Scrambled Eggs 36
Tofu with Miso Sauce 37
Eggplant Wrapped in Miso Pork 38
Chicken Spring Rolls with Miso 39

Main Dishes

Chicken Karaage with Miso 41
Stir-fried Pork with Miso 42
Miso Chicken Patties 43
Sea Bream with Miso and Butter 44
Chicken in Sesame Miso 45
Cabbage and Pork Hot Pot with Miso 46
Miso-flavored Gyoza Dumplings 49
Broccoli and Bacon Miso Gratin 50
Chunky Vegetable Miso Stew 52
Miso Bulgogi with Ginger 53
Miso Carbonara 55
Miso Hayashi Rice 56
Miso Butter Chicken Curry 57
Miso Soy Milk Tantanmen 58
Chilled Udon Noodles with Chicken 59
Chicken and Lotus Root Rice with Miso 60
Fried Rice with Miso and Pickles 61

Pickles and Marinades

Pan-fried Pork Marinated in Miso 63
Grilled Salmon Marinated in Miso 64
Cucumber and Turnip Miso Pickles 65

Everyday Sides

Carrot with Walnuts 66
Chicken with Lotus Root 66
Miso Kinpira 67
Greens with Miso and Tofu 67
Cucumber with Vinegar Miso 68
Korean-style Miso Bell Pepper Namul 68
Miso Potatoes 69
Daikon Stewed in Miso 69

Dressings, Sauces and Dips

Miso Dressing 70
Umeboshi Miso Dressing 70
Onion Miso Dressing 70
Chinese Ginger Dressing 70
Sesame Miso Sauce 71
Gochujang Miso Sauce 71
Miso Sauce with Onion 71
Walnut and Miso Dip 72
Cheesy Miso Dip 72

Sweet Treats with Miso

Miso Ice Cream 74
Kinako Miso Truffles 75
Miso Sesame Cookies 76
Miso Cheesecake 77
Miso Milk Pudding 78
Ma Lai Go Sponge Cake with Miso 79
Miso Banana Bread 80

Fermented Seasonings

Shio Koji 82
Shoyu Koji 84
Fish Sauce Koji 85
Easy Gochujang Korean Chili Paste 86
Amazake 87
Traditional Miso 88

Glossary of Ingredients 90
Index of Main Ingredients 94

An Easy Way to Enhance Every Meal!

"What's your favorite food?" As I work in this field, I am asked this question a lot. But there are so many dishes I like that it's really hard to pick one. If pressed, though, I would probably say miso soup. This soup is such an integral part of Japanese people's lives that we take it for granted, but it actually a remarkably potent superfood. It's even said that "miso keeps the doctor away," thanks to its impressive health benefits.

The usual fermentation process for making miso takes from six months to up to a year or more. But wanting to incorporate more miso into my life, I came up with my own method of making homemade miso that can be ready in *just one night*! In addition to the 87 miso-based recipes you'll find in this book, you'll also find instructions for how to make your own miso overnight using the keep-warm function of a rice cooker (you can also use a yogurt maker, slow cooker or sous vide machine, see note on page 11), which activates the enzymes needed for fermentation. This means that miso, which normally takes more than six months to make, can be ready overnight.

This speedy method is ideal for people who want to make miso at home for the first time, or who want to make it quickly, or who simply want a foolproof method for making it frequently. It's made using extra amounts of rice koji, which has a gentle sweetness and a comforting flavor. I don't use much salt, so you can use lots of homemade miso in your cooking to make nutritious and tasty dishes easily—Japanese or Western—without worrying about having too much salt in your food.

All the recipes in this book make use of my recipe for homemade miso on page 10, and I hope you will try to make it yourself. But the recipes can also be made with store-bought white miso. Whether you use homemade miso or ready-made white miso, I hope that this book will help you incorporate this delicious, health-giving food into your daily diet!

—Misa Enomoto

All About Homemade Miso

Homemade Miso is not just quick and easy to make — it is an especially beneficial fermented food with a different umami and sweetness to typical store-bought miso. It brings out the best flavors in your dishes and nourishes your body from the inside out.

What Makes Homemade Miso So Delicious?

Adds Umami
During the fermentation process, the protein in soybeans breaks down into glutamic acid and other substances. As you may know, glutamic acid is a key source of umami. Homemade Miso is low in salt and can be used generously to enhance the umami of dishes and make them more delicious.

Adds Flavor
Homemade Miso combines a strong umami flavor, natural sweetness, and just the right touch of saltiness. When you skillfully pair it with the flavors of other ingredients, you can create a well-balanced and satisfying dish without needing to use a lot of additional seasonings.

Tenderizes Meat and Fish
Homemade Miso contains more of the enzymes derived from rice koji (see page 10). One of these enzymes, protease, has the ability to break down proteins. So when you use miso with meat or fish, their protein is broken down and they become more tender.

Adds Sweetness
One of the enzymes derived from the rice koji used to make Homemade Miso is amylase, which converts starch into glucose and oligosaccharides, creating a gentle sweetness. Because Homemade Miso contains a high proportion of rice koji, you can add even more of this natural sweetness when you use it in your cooking.

Adds Just the Right Amount of Saltiness
Homemade Miso contains much less salt—about 5%—compared to regular miso, which typically has around 10%. This means you can use it more generously without making your dishes too salty, allowing you to create meals that are packed with miso's rich umami and nutrients.

Goes Well with Western Food
One of the characteristics of Homemade Miso is that it goes well with dairy products such as cheese and milk, so it's a great complement to Western-style dishes as well as Japanese ones. With a little creativity, you can expand your recipe repertoire and bring more variety and color to your daily meals.

What Are the Health Benefits of Homemade Miso?

A Source of Good Bacteria
Homemade Miso is rich in oligosaccharides, which serve as nourishment for the good bacteria in your gut. In addition, rice koji and soybeans contain dietary fiber, which not only feeds helpful gut bacteria, but helps relieve constipation and supports the smooth elimination of waste, promoting a balanced and healthy digestive system.

Helps Control Blood Pressure
Homemade Miso contains soy isoflavones. Isoflavones have been shown to help suppress increases in blood pressure and blood cholesterol levels. Because Homemade Miso is also low in salt, it is a good choice for people who are concerned about their blood pressure.

Gives Skin a Healthy Glow
Soy isoflavones act in the body in a way similar to the female hormone estrogen, thought to promote the production of collagen, which helps give the skin firmness and luster. Kojic acid, produced by koji, is also believed to have a brightening effect on the skin.

Relieves Stress
Because Homemade Miso contains a higher amount of koji, it has much more GABA—a natural amino acid that helps calm the nervous system—than regular miso. GABA works to reduce tension and mental stress and has a relaxing effect. It is also believed to help keep blood pressure from rising.

Boosts Immunity
Miso has strong antioxidant properties that help protect the body from harmful substances that can damage cells and weaken the immune system. The dietary fiber and beneficial bacteria in miso stimulate the intestines, where many immune cells are located, helping to strengthen immunity and support the body's natural defenses against infection.

Prevents Aging
Homemade Miso contains abundant antioxidants such as soybean saponins, isoflavones and vitamin E. These help protect the body from damage that can lead to aging, and are believed to support staying youthful and healthy. Kojic acid also has protective, anti-aging properties.

Gives Energy
Homemade Miso is rich in B vitamins, which play a role in the metabolism of proteins and carbohydrates, helping convert nutrients from food into energy efficiently. Isoflavones and antioxidants such as vitamin E also support recovery from fatigue.

Lowers Blood Cholesterol
Homemade Miso contains a lot of unsaturated fatty acids such as linoleic acid. Unsaturated fatty acids are believed to lower blood cholesterol. Natural compounds from soybeans called saponins may also help keep cholesterol from rising too high.

Nutrients in Homemade Miso

Homemade Miso is packed with essential amino acids that your body needs to stay healthy. It also offers a wealth of other nutrients that are great for overall wellness. Adding miso to your everyday meals is a simple way to help keep you and your family feeling your best.

Protein

In Japan soybeans are sometimes referred to as "meat of the field"—this is because they are naturally rich in protein. Even better, the protein in soybeans is high quality, containing a well-balanced mix of essential amino acids. Pairing soy-based food with rice is a great way to boost the overall protein content of your meal.

Dietary Fiber

Dietary fiber can help to relieve constipation and to keep your digestive system in good shape. Because so many immune cells are found in the gut, taking care of your digestion can also help strengthen your immune system. Plus, fiber can help prevent sharp spikes in blood sugar after meals and reduce the amount of cholesterol your body absorbs, which may lower the risk of lifestyle-related diseases over time.

B Vitamins

B vitamins—like B1, B2, niacin, and pantothenic acid—are important nutrients that mainly help your body's metabolism. They quickly convert carbohydrates and fats into energy, support healthy circulation, aid recovery from fatigue and help build resilience to stress. Because B vitamins are water-soluble and aren't stored in the body, it's important to include them regularly in your meals.

Healthy Fats

The fats in soybeans are rich in essential fatty acids like linoleic acid and alpha-linolenic acid, which your body needs to get from food. These healthy fats can help lower cholesterol levels. Alpha-linolenic acid also plays a role in making DHA, a type of omega-3 fat that supports brain health, and EPA, another omega-3 that helps improve circulation and reduce inflammation.

Enzymes

Enzymes like amylase and protease are essential for breaking down carbohydrates and proteins. Carbohydrates are turned into sugars, and proteins are broken down into amino acids, making them easier for your body to digest and absorb. These sugars add sweetness, while the amino acids create savory depth and umami. That's one of the reasons Homemade Miso has such a rich, delicious flavor.

Antioxidants

Soy saponins, isoflavones, and vitamin E found in miso are antioxidants that help protect your body from the damage caused by free radicals. These nutrients can help slow down cell aging, support healthy skin, and strengthen your immune system. Including miso regularly in your diet is a great way to help keep your body strong, resilient and youthful.

Iron and Folic Acid

Iron is a component of hemoglobin in the blood and plays an important role in carrying oxygen through the body. When you don't get enough iron, you may feel tired more easily and have a weaker immune system. Folic acid is a B vitamin that supports the production of healthy red blood cells, helps prevent anemia, and promotes cell growth. It's especially important for pregnant and breastfeeding women to get enough folic acid in their diet.

Kojic Acid

Kojic acid, which is produced during fermentation, helps block the formation of melanin, the pigment that can cause dark spots. That's why it's also used as an ingredient in brightening skincare products. Kojic acid may also help protect your skin from damage caused by UV rays, which can lead to wrinkles and sagging. It's a great nutrient if you're concerned about keeping your skin healthy and clear.

How to Make Homemade Miso Overnight

Homemade Miso is made using the keep-warm setting on a rice cooker. Because the fermentation is finished in just one night, you can make it whenever you like and always enjoy it fresh. It's easy for anyone to make — so please give it a try!

MAKES ABOUT 2 LBS 2 OZ (1 KG)

1 cup (200 g) dried soybeans
1 lb 2 oz (500 g) fresh rice koji
3 tablespoons (50 g) salt

Rice koji is steamed rice inoculated with koji fungus and Aspergillus oryzae (lactic acid bacteria), which enhances fermentation and flavor. You can find it sold fresh or dried at Japanese or Asian markets or online.

1 Soak the soybeans
Put the soybeans in a large bowl, with about 8¼ cups (2 L) of water to cover, and soak for at least 18 hours until the soybeans have doubled in size. In hot weather, keep the bowl in the refrigerator while soaking.

2 Boil the soybeans
Drain the soaked soybeans and transfer to a heavy pot. Add enough fresh water to cover the beans. Bring to a boil over medium-high heat, then skim off any foam that rises to the surface. Turn the heat to medium-low and simmer for 3–4 hours, stirring occasionally to prevent sticking. If more foam appears, skim it off. Add more water as needed to keep the beans covered while they cook.

When you can crush a soybean between your thumb and little finger, they are cooked. Drain in colander, reserving the cooking water.

3 Crush the rice koji and salt
Put the rice koji in a food processor and crush into a fine powder (this makes it easier to ferment). Add the salt and mix. Transfer to a bowl.

> *If you don't have a food processor for Steps 3–5, roughly chop the rice koji with a knife and mash the soybeans by hand.
> *If you have equipment that can hold a steady temperature of about 140°F (60°C), such as a yogurt maker, slow cooker, or sous vide machine, you can ferment the miso in the same amount of time.
> *Because rice cooker models vary, please check the instruction manual in advance. Also, please be careful not to burn yourself while keeping the rice warm.

4 Mash the soybeans
Put the soybeans in the food processor (no need to wash it) and mash. Let the mash cool down enough to handle (the enzymes stop working above 140°F [60°C]).

5 Mix together
Mix the Step 4 mash with the rice koji. Use your hands, breaking up any lumps. Add some of the reserved cooking water (see note, facing page) a little at a time. Mix until everything is combined.

6 Put into a rice cooker
Take out an amount you can hold in one hand and roll into a ball, pressing gently to remove any air. Place in the rice cooker pot. Continue packing the remaining mixture in the same way until all of it is used.

*The amount of water used in Step 5 should be a little over ½ cup (130m); or a little more if using dried rice koji, but this will vary depending on the texture of the soybeans and koji. Adjust the amount of water as needed—the mixture should be just a little more moist than finished miso.

*Tip: The leftover cooking liquid is rich in nutrients from the soybeans, so don't throw it out! See page 16 for ideas on how to use it.

7 Keep warm overnight

Place the inner pot back into the rice cooker. Drape a damp kitchen towel over the top, folded in half so it's doubled. Leave the lid open, and set the cooker to the "Keep Warm" setting.

8 Done

Let it sit for 6 to 8 hours. When it's done, give the miso a gentle stir with a wooden spatula or spoon—that's it! Your fresh miso is ready to use.

Transfer the miso to a clean storage container. You can start enjoying it right away. Keeps one month refrigerated.

Homemade Miso Made with Other Beans

You can make Homemade Miso with beans other than soybeans. Try using green soybeans or black soybeans for a different flavor. You can even use adzuki beans, which don't need soaking, or okara (soybean pulp), which skips the step of boiling beans altogether. Have fun experimenting to discover your favorite taste and aroma!

Adzuki Bean Miso

Chickpea Miso

Adzuki Bean Miso

Can be made without soaking.

MAKES ABOUT 2 LBS 2 OZ (1 KG)

1 lb 2 oz (500 g) fresh rice koji
½ cup (100 g) dried adzuki beans, briefly rinsed
3 tablespoons (50 g) salt

1. Bring 2½ cups (600 ml) of water to a boil in a heavy pot, add the adzuki beans, and when the pot comes back to a boil, add ¾ cup (200 ml) of water. When it comes to a boil again, simmer over medium heat for about 10 minutes. Cover, turn off the heat, and let it steam for 30 minutes. Drain and rinse briefly.
2. Follow Steps 2 to 8 of the Homemade Miso recipe (see page 10). In Step 2, use 2½ cups (600 ml) of water and simmer for 50 minutes.

At the end of Step 1, rinse briefly to wash away the scum.

Green Soybean Miso

Made with fragrant green soybeans.

MAKES ABOUT 2 LBS 2 OZ (1 KG)

1 cup (200 g) dried green soybeans
1 lb 2 oz (500 g) fresh rice koji
3 tablespoons (50 g) salt

1. Follow the recipe for Homemade Miso (see page 10).

Chickpea Miso

Has a rich and mellow flavor.

MAKES ABOUT 2 LBS 2 OZ (1 KG)

1 cup (200 g) dried chickpeas
1 lb 2 oz (500 g) fresh rice koji
3 tablespoons (50 g) salt

1. Follow the recipe for Homemade Miso (page 10). For Step 1, soak the chickpeas for at least 10 hours, and for Step 2, simmer the chickpeas for 2–3 hours.

Black Soybean Miso

The cooking liquid is also full of nutrients.

MAKES ABOUT 2 LBS 2 OZ (1 KG)

1 cup (200 g) dried black soybeans
1 lb 2 oz (500 g) fresh rice koji
3 tablespoons (50 g) salt

1. Soak and boil the soybeans in the same way as Steps 1 and 2 of Homemade Miso (page 10). The water used to soak the black soybeans will be rich in anthocyanins (natural antioxidants), so use the soaking water for boiling too.
2. Follow Steps 3–8 of Homemade Miso (see page 10).

To avoid staining your pot, transfer the beans into the pot only after they have been soaked.

Okara Miso

No need to boil beans for this hassle-free miso made with soy bean pulp.

MAKES ABOUT 2 LBS 2 OZ (1 KG)

1 lb 2 oz (500 g) fresh rice koji
3 tablespoons (50 g) salt
10 oz (300 g) fresh okara soybean pulp

1. Crush the koji to a fine powder in a food processor. Mix in the salt, then transfer to a bowl.
2. Put the okara and 1¼ cups (300 ml) of water into a pot over low heat. Stir until the temperature reaches 122°F (50°C). Add to the Step 1 bowl and mix with your hands, breaking up any lumps. (If using dried rice koji, also add 6½ tablespoons of water.)
3. Follow Steps 6–8 of Homemade Miso (see page 10).

If the temperature is too low or too high, fermentation won't work well. Warm the mixture to about 122°F (50°C); it should be slightly hot to the touch.

All About Homemade Miso

Homemade Miso Q & A

Here you'll find answers to common questions, plus a few handy tips to make the process smoother. Take a moment to read this section before you get started.

Q When is the best time of year to make miso?
A You can make it at any time of year.
The traditional method of fermenting miso at room temperature is best done in winter to avoid the mold that can appear in warm weather. Homemade Miso, however, is ready after one night, so there is no danger of mold. This means you can make it at any time.

Q Can I make miso with dried rice koji?
A Absolutely!
Dried koji is easier to find than fresh koji. Just add a bit more of the cooking liquid when you mix it in, and follow the same steps as you would with fresh koji. If you'd like to try fresh koji, you can find it at health-food stores, Japanese markets, sake breweries, or online retailers.

Q What kind of salt is best for making miso?
A I recommend using coarse salt.
You can use any kind of salt, but I recommend coarse salt as it gives a good flavor and a mild finish.

Q How do I store miso? How long does it keep?
A It keeps for about a month in the refrigerator.
Homemade Miso has less salt than regular miso, so it doesn't keep as long, but it keeps for about a month in a clean container in the refrigerator. Freshly made miso is delicious, so eat it sooner rather than later!

Q Can I close the rice cooker lid?
A You should keep the lid open.
To maintain the right temperature of around 140°F (60°C), you should leave the lid open. Rice cookers have a keep-warm setting of around 158°F (70°C). This is too hot and stops the enzymes in the koji from working. Leave the lid open and cover the top with a damp cloth to stop the miso drying out. This keeps the temperature at the ideal level for fermentation.

Q Can I use the water left over from boiling beans?
A Yes—it's full of nutrients and very versatile.

The cooking liquid from soybeans, green soybeans or chickpeas can be diluted with an equal amount of water and used as a flavorful broth base for miso soup. If you've cooked black soybeans or adzuki beans, the liquid makes a delicious tea—enjoy it as is, or mix it with soy milk or regular milk for a latte-style drink. You can add a little honey or raw sugar.

Q Can miso only be made with freshly cooked soybeans?
A No, you can use precooked soybeans.

Cooked soybeans, and their cooking liquid can be frozen. Just separate the beans and the liquid into different freezer-safe resealable bags, seal well, and store in the freezer. This way, you can cook a large batch when you have time and have everything ready to make miso whenever you like. When you're ready to use them, thaw the soybeans, then steam for 10 minutes before mixing. Bring the cooking liquid to a boil before using it.

Homemade Miso Makes the Best Miso Soup!

Homemade Miso is rich in sweetness and umami. If you want to enjoy its flavor in the simplest, most delicious way, miso soup is the way to go. Because this miso has less salt than regular varieties, you can use a generous amount without worrying about it being too salty—and you'll get even more of the health benefits of fermented food. Add seasonal vegetables for a comforting, nourishing bowl that will leave you completely satisfied.

Onion and Carrot Miso Soup with Ginger

The natural sweetness of vegetables and the warmth of fresh ginger make a soothing bowl that warms you from the inside out.

SERVES 2

- 1¾ cups (400 ml) dashi stock
- ¼ onion, thinly sliced lengthwise
- ¼ carrot, sliced ⅛ inch (3 mm) thick and quartered
- 1 piece ginger, finely shredded
- 3 tablespoons Homemade Miso (page 10), or white miso

1. Bring the dashi stock to a gentle boil in a pot over medium heat, add the onion and carrot, cover with a lid, and simmer for 3–4 minutes.
2. Add the ginger and turn the heat to low. Dissolve the miso in a ladleful of the cooking liquid, add to the pan and stir.

Warm up your body from the inside out and boost your immunity

Packed with isoflavones, especially beneficial for women!

Leek and Tofu Miso Soup

Chunks of leek are simmered until soft and sweet. The combination of miso and tofu gives you a double dose of the goodness of soybeans.

SERVES 2

½ block atsu-age deep-fried tofu, about 3 oz (75 g)
1 leek or fat green onion
1¾ cups (400 ml) dashi stock
3 tablespoons Homemade Miso (page 10), or white miso

1. Cut the tofu into long strips then cut each strip into ½ inch (1 cm) pieces. Cut the leek into 1 inch (2.5 cm) pieces.
2. Bring the dashi to a gentle boil in a pot over medium heat, add the leeks and fried tofu, cover and simmer for 5–6 minutes. Turn the heat to low. Dissolve the miso in a ladleful of the cooking liquid, add to the pan and stir.

Sake Lees Soup with Salmon and Taro

Sake lees are the creamy, nutrient-rich solids left over from sake production. They add subtle sweetness and richness to dishes. You can find sake lees at Japanese grocery stores or online.

SERVES 2

3½ oz (100 g) piece fresh salmon
2 taro roots
1½ oz (40 g) pressed sake lees
1¾ cups (400 ml) dashi stock
3 tablespoons Overnight Miso, or white miso

1. Cut the salmon into 4 equal pieces. Peel the taro roots and cut into ¼ inch (5 mm) thick slices.
2. Put the sake lees in a microwave-safe bowl and sprinkle with 1 tablespoon of water. Cover loosely with plastic wrap, microwave for 40 seconds, then mix well. (See note about microwaving, page 59.)
3. Combine the dashi stock and the sake lees in a pot, add the taro, cover and bring to a gentle boil over medium heat. Lower the heat, simmer for about 5 minutes, add the salmon, cover again and simmer for a further 3 minutes. Dissolve the miso in a ladleful of the cooking liquid, add to the pan and stir.

A warming bowl to fight the chill—great for anti-aging, too!

Pork and Root Vegetable Miso Soup

This hearty serving of fiber-rich root vegetables tastes even better the next day as the flavors soak in. A sprinkle of shichimi togarashi—a Japanese seven-spice blend—adds a kick.

SERVES 4

5½ oz (150 g) thinly sliced pork
1 inch (2–3 cm) thick slice daikon radish
¼ carrot
½ burdock root
2 teaspoons sesame oil
1 piece ginger, shredded
½ leek or fat green onion, thinly sliced diagonally
3¼ cups (800 ml) dashi stock
6 tablespoons Overnight Miso, or white miso
Shichimi togarashi, to serve

1. Cut the pork slices into 1 inch (3 cm) pieces. Cut the daikon into ¼ inch (5mm) slices, and quarter each slice. Cut the carrot in half lengthways, and cut into ⅛ inch (3 mm) slices. Peel and thinly shave the burdock root.

2. Heat the sesame oil and ginger in a pot over medium heat. Stir-fry the daikon, carrot, burdock and leek until wilted. Add the pork and stir-fry until the color changes.

3. Add the dashi stock, bring to a gentle boil, then turn the heat to medium-low. Cover, and simmer for about 10 minutes. Turn the heat to low, dissolve the miso in a ladleful of the cooking liquid, add to the pan and stir. Serve sprinkled with shichimi togarashi.

Supports digestion and helps keep skin clear

Chicken and Cabbage Miso Soup

Chicken is full of umami, so there's no need for stock. Yuzu kosho citrus-chili paste adds a kick.

SERVES 2

3½ oz (100 g) boneless chicken thigh
1 napa cabbage leaf, cut crosswise into ½ inch (1.5 cm) strips
3 tablespoons Homemade Miso (page 10), or white miso
Yuzu kosho, to serve

1. Cut the chicken into bite-size pieces.
2. Put the chicken in a pot with 1¼ cups (300 ml) of water and bring to a gentle boil over medium-low heat. Add the cabbage, cover, and simmer for 3–4 minutes. Turn the heat to low, dissolve the miso in a ladleful of the cooking liquid, add to the pan and stir. Serve topped with yuzu kosho.

Miso Soup with Yam and Seaweed

Nagaimo is a type of Japanese yam that becomes slippery and sticky when grated, to create a smooth, comforting soup.

SERVES 2

1¾ cups (400 ml) dashi stock
5½ oz (150 g) Japanese nagaimo yam, grated
3 tablespoons Homemade Miso (page 10), or white miso
1 small handful aosa seaweed
Small piece ginger, cut into matchsticks

1. Bring the dashi stock to a gentle boil in a pot over medium heat, then add the grated yam. When the pot comes back to a gentle boil, turn the heat to low. Dissolve the miso in a ladleful of the cooking liquid, and mix it in to the pot with the aosa seaweed. Serve garnished with the ginger.

Spicy Miso Soup with Pea Shoots

The spiciness is good for blood circulation. The sesame seeds add a savory flavor and minerals.

SERVES 2

1 teaspoon sesame oil
½ cup (80 g) napa cabbage kimchi, chopped
1¾ cups (400 ml) dashi stock
Small bunch pea shoots, about 2 oz (50 g), halved
3 tablespoons Homemade Miso (page 10), or white miso
2 teaspoons ground sesame seeds

1. Heat the sesame oil in a pot over medium heat. Add the kimchi and sauté briefly.
2. Add the dashi, bring to a gentle boil, add the pea shoots, and lower the heat to a gentle simmer. Dissolve the miso in a ladle of cooking liquid, add to the pan and stir. Stir in the sesame seeds.

Miso Soup with Komatsuna Greens and Egg

This mild-tasting soup is packed with nutritious eggs and greens. If you can't find komatsuna, try baby spinach.

SERVES 2

3½ oz (100 g) komatsuna greens
1¾ cups (400 ml) dashi stock
2 eggs, beaten
3½ tablespoons Homemade Miso (page 10), or white miso

1. Cut the komatsuna into 1 inch (3 cm) pieces.
2. Bring the dashi stock to a gentle boil in a pot over medium heat, and add the komatsuna. When the pot returns to a gentle boil, pour in the beaten egg in a circular motion. When the egg floats to the top, stir it in. Turn the heat to low, dissolve the miso in a ladleful of the cooking liquid, add to the pan and stir.

Miso Soup with Turnip and Baby Sardines

Using the turnip leaves as well as the root adds extra vitamins. Turnip pairs well with baby sardines.

SERVES 2

1 small Asian turnip, about 3 oz (80 g), with greens
1¾ cups (400 ml) dashi stock
3 tablespoons Homemade Miso (page 10), or white miso
2 tablespoons shirasu-boshi baby sardines

1. Cut the turnip greens into ½ inch (1.5 cm) pieces. Cut the turnip into ½ inch cubes.
2. Bring the dashi stock to a gentle boil in a pot over medium heat, add the turnip cubes and simmer for about 3 minutes. Add the turnip greens, simmer for another 1 or 2 minutes, then turn the heat to low. Dissolve the miso in a ladleful of the cooking liquid, add to the pan and stir. Serve topped with the shirasu-boshi.

Cabbage and Shrimp Miso Soup

Tender simmered cabbage is easy on the stomach. Adding dried sakura shrimp makes this soup a great source of calcium, too.

SERVES 2

1¾ cups (400 ml) dashi stock
1 large cabbage leaf, about 3½ oz (100 g), roughly chopped
3 tablespoons Homemade Miso (page 10), or white miso
2 tablespoons dried sakura shrimp

1. Bring the dashi stock to a gentle boil in a pot over medium heat, add the cabbage, cover, and simmer for 3–4 minutes. Turn the heat to low. Dissolve the miso in a ladleful of the cooking liquid, add to the pan and with the sakura shrimp and stir.

Miso Soup with Asparagus and Onion

Olive oil helps your body absorb more beta-carotene. This soup pairs wonderfully with Western-style meals.

SERVES 2

2 green asparagus stalks
2 teaspoons olive oil + extra for drizzling
¼ onion, sliced thinly lengthwise
1¾ cups (400 ml) dashi stock
3 tablespoons Homemade Miso (page 10), or white miso

1. Peel the root ends of the asparagus stalks, and cut the stalks into 2 inch (5 cm) pieces.
2. Heat the olive oil in a pot over medium heat, and stir-fry the onion until soft. Add the dashi stock, bring to a gentle boil, then add the asparagus and cook for about 1 minute. Turn the heat to low, dissolve the miso in a ladleful of the cooking liquid, add to the pan and stir. Serve drizzled with a little olive oil, if you like.

Green Pepper and Pork Miso Soup

The mild bitterness of green peppers adds a fresh twist. They also contain nutrients that help support recovery from fatigue.

SERVES 2

3 oz (80 g) thinly sliced pork belly
2 small green bell peppers
1 teaspoon sesame oil
1 piece ginger, peeled and shredded
1¾ cups (400 ml) dashi stock
3 tablespoons Homemade Miso (page 10), or white miso
Japanese karashi mustard, to serve

1. Cut the pork into 1 inch (3 cm) pieces. Halve the peppers and cut into ¼ inch (5 mm) strips.
2. Heat the sesame oil and ginger in a pot over medium heat. When fragrant, add the pork and stir-fry until it changes color. Add the peppers, stir-fry briefly, then add the dashi stock and bring to a gentle boil. Lower the heat, dissolve the miso in a ladleful of the cooking liquid, add to the pan and stir. Serve topped with a little mustard.

Miso Soup with Eggplant

The sweetness of the miso goes well with the fried eggplant. The fresh aroma of myoga ginger makes this soup especially appetizing.

SERVES 2

1 Asian eggplant
1 tablespoon sesame oil
1¾ cups (400 ml) dashi stock
3 tablespoons Homemade Miso (page 10), or white miso
1 myoga ginger bud, thinly sliced thinly

1. Halve the eggplant, cut each half into 3 pieces horizontally, and make shallow diagonal cuts in the surface of each piece.
2. Heat the sesame oil in a pot over medium heat, and add the eggplant, skin side down. Brown the eggplant on both sides, turn off the heat and wipe out excess oil from the pot. Add the dashi stock, bring to a gentle boil, then lower the heat. Dissolve the miso in a ladle of the cooking liquid, add to the pan and stir. Serve topped with myoga.

Mushroom Miso Soup

A bowl full of umami. The combination of mushrooms and miso helps to support healthy digestion.

SERVES 2

3½ oz (100 g) shimeji mushrooms
2 oz (50 g) maitake mushrooms
1 tablespoon sesame oil
½ red chili pepper, thinly sliced
1¾ cups (400 ml) dashi stock
3 tablespoons Homemade Miso (page 10), or white miso
Green part of a scallion, thinly sliced

1. Pull the mushrooms apart into small clumps.
2. Heat sesame oil in a pot over medium heat, and fry the shimeji mushrooms, maitake mushrooms and red chili pepper until soft. Add the dashi stock and bring to a gentle boil, then lower the heat. Dissolve the miso in a ladleful of the cooking liquid, add to the pan and stir. Serve garnished with the scallion.

Yam and Okra Miso Soup

Enjoy the light, velvety broth and the crisp texture of the vegetables. This soup is also packed with plenty of fiber.

SERVES 2

1¾ cups (400 ml) dashi stock
3½ oz (100 g) Japanese nagaimo yam (put into a plastic bag and bash into fairly large pieces with a rolling pin)
2 okra, thinly sliced thinly
3 tablespoons Homemade Miso (page 10), or white miso

1. Bring the dashi stock to a gentle boil in a pot over medium heat, then add the yam and okra and cook for 1–2 minutes, then turn the heat to low. Dissolve the miso in a ladleful of the cooking liquid, add to the pan and stir.

Miso Soup with Cauliflower

The sweetness of miso goes well with cauliflower. Adding sesame seeds boosts both flavor and health benefits.

SERVES 2

1¾ cups (400 ml) dashi stock
¼ cauliflower, about 3½ oz (100 g); divided into florets that are cut in half
1 tablespoon ground sesame seeds + more for sprinkling
3 tablespoons Homemade Miso (page 10), or white miso

1. Bring the dashi stock to a gentle boil in a pot over medium heat, then add the cauliflower. Cover and simmer for 2–3 minutes, then turn the heat to low, and add the ground sesame seeds. Dissolve the miso in a ladleful of the cooking liquid, add to the pan and stir. Serve sprinkled with ground sesame seeds.

Tomato and Bacon Soup

The umami and acidity of the tomato goes well with the sweetness of the miso.

SERVES 2

½ tomato
1 slice bacon
1 teaspoon olive oil
1¾ cups (400 ml) dashi stock
3 tablespoons Homemade Miso (page 10), or white miso
Coarsely ground black pepper, to taste

1. Cut the tomato and the bacon into ½ inch (1 cm) dice.
2. Heat the olive oil in a pot over medium heat, and briefly fry the bacon. Add the dashi stock and bring to a gentle boil. Add the tomato and turn the heat to low. Dissolve the miso in a ladleful of the cooking liquid, add to the pan and stir. Serve sprinkled with black pepper.

Kabocha Miso Soup

A quick and easy potage made with kabocha squash, which contains vitamins A, C and E.

SERVES 2

3½ oz (100 g) kabocha squash
¼ onion
2 teaspoons olive oil
¾ cup (200 ml) dashi stock
¾ cup (200 ml) milk
3 tablespoons Homemade Miso (page 10), or white miso
Roasted black sesame seeds, to serve

1. Cut the kabocha squash into bite-size pieces about ½ inch (8 mm) thick. Cut the onion into ¼ inch (5 mm) dice.
2. Heat the olive oil in a pot over medium heat, and fry the onion and pumpkin until soft. Add the dashi stock and milk, cover with a lid, and simmer over low heat for about 5 minutes.
3. Roughly mash the kabocha squash. Dissolve the miso in a ladleful of the cooking liquid, add to the pan and stir. Serve sprinkled with the sesame seeds.

Potato and Corn Miso Soup with Soy Milk

Soy milk and Homemade Miso go together very well. The natural sweetness of this soup is very comforting.

SERVES 2

1¾ cups (400 ml) dashi stock
1 potato, about 5½ oz (150 g), cut into 8 pieces
6½ tablespoons soy milk
3 tablespoons whole corn kernels
3 tablespoons Homemade Miso (page 10), or white miso

1. Put the dashi stock and potato in a pot and cover with a lid. Bring to a gentle boil over medium heat. Turn the heat to medium-low and simmer for 8–10 minutes. Add the soy milk and warm it through, then add the corn. Dissolve the miso in a ladleful of the cooking liquid, add to the pan and stir.

Fermented foods + vitamin C = a powerful combo for clear and healthy skin

Instant Miso Soup

Just put everything in a cup, add boiling water and you're done! With the umami of Homemade Miso and the flavorful ingredients, these soups are delicious even without dashi stock.

Wakame and Fu Instant Miso Soup

These two simple ingredients—*fu* wheat gluten and dried wakame seaweed—make a delicious miso soup.

SERVES 2

Dried wakame seaweed, cut in small pieces, about 1 teaspoon
6 pieces ball-shaped fu wheat gluten
3 tablespoons Homemade Miso (page 10), or white miso

1. Divide the seaweed, fu wheat gluten and miso equally between two cups. Pour ⅔ cup (150 ml) boiling water into each and stir.

Fu is dried wheat gluten. When rehydrated, it is soft and slightly chewy, absorbing the flavors of soups and broths.

Nori and Sesame Instant Miso Soup

The aroma of the sea combines with the warm, nutty scent of sesame. So flavorful, you'd never guess it's instant!

SERVES 2

3 tablespoons Homemade Miso (page 10), or white miso
½ sheet nori seaweed, 4 x 3½ inches (10 x 9 cm)
Roasted white sesame seeds, for garnish

1. Divide the miso equally between two cups, pour ⅔ cup (150 ml) of boiling water into each and mix. Tear up the nori and divide between each cup. Crush the roasted sesame seeds between your fingers and sprinkle them on top.

Kombu and Umeboshi Instant Miso Soup

The soft, velvety texture of the tororo kombu (shredded kelp) gives a comforting texture, and the tart pickled plum adds zing.

SERVES 2

3 tablespoons Homemade Miso (page 10), or white miso
2 pinches tororo kombu
1 umeboshi plum

1. Divide the miso equally between two cups, pour ⅔ cup (150 ml) of boiling water into each and mix. Add a pinch of tororo kombu to each one. Break the umeboshi into pieces and add to the cups.

Mitsuba and Ginger Instant Miso Soup

Mitsuba is a Japanese herb with a crisp, parsley-like flavor.

SERVES 2

3 tablespoons Homemade Miso (page 10), or white miso
4–5 stalks mitsuba, roughly chopped
1 teaspoon grated ginger

1. Divide the miso equally between two cups, pour ⅔ cup (150 ml) of boiling water into each and mix. Add the mitsuba and ginger to each cup.

Myoga and Shiso Instant Miso Soup

Aromatic vegetables take center stage in a fragrant soup that is perfect for summer.

SERVES 2

3 tablespoons Homemade Miso (page 10), or white miso
½ myoga ginger bud, thinly sliced
1 green shiso leaf

1. Divide the miso equally between two cups, pour ⅔ cup (150 ml) of boiling water into each and mix. Add the myoga ginger and torn up shiso leaf to each cup.

Delicious Everyday Dishes with Homemade Miso

Homemade Miso, which brings out the deep umami of soybeans, is perfect for everyday cooking. It enhances the natural flavor of ingredients, and when combined with other seasonings, it works beautifully, not only in Japanese recipes but also in Western-style dishes. It's also great as a marinade base or for making pickles.

Simply Seasoned Snacks

Homemade Miso is low in salt and has a natural sweetness, which makes it a perfect seasoning ingredient. You can use it generously, and it's great for your health, too!

Miso Butter Toast

Miso and butter go well together. Because this is low in salt, you can spread it on generously and it won't be salty.

SERVES 2

2 slices bread
2 tablespoons Homemade Miso (page 10), or white miso
Butter, to taste
Shredded nori seaweed, to taste

1. Spread the bread evenly with the miso, and toast in a toaster oven until browned. If toasting under a grill, toast one side of the bread, then turn the bread over, spread with miso, and toast that side. Top with butter and nori seaweed while still hot.

Miso Rice Balls with Shiso

Miso is mixed with shiso leaves and grilled until golden brown, creating an irresistible aroma and taste.

SERVES 2

1½ cups (300 g) warm cooked medium-grain Japonica rice
3 tablespoons Homemade Miso (page 10), or white miso
2 green shiso leaves, minced
Sesame oil, for brushing

1. Divide the rice into four equal portions and form into balls.
2. Mix the miso with the minced shiso and spread evenly over one side of each rice ball. Place the rice balls on a grill rack, brush lightly with sesame oil and grill for about 4 minutes.

Miso Grilled Turnip

The sweet, juicy turnip, grilled to perfection, goes well with the savory miso.

SERVES 2

1½ tablespoons Homemade Miso (page 10), or white miso
1 Asian turnip, sliced unpeeled into 4 equal rounds
Sansho pepper powder, to taste

1. Spread the miso evenly over each slice of turnip. Grill for 5–6 minutes. Serve sprinkled with sansho pepper.

Delicious Everyday Dishes

Miso Scrambled Eggs

The gentle sweetness of miso pairs perfectly with eggs. It adds a rich, savory flavor to your everyday egg dishes.

SERVES 2

2 teaspoons vegetable oil
2 eggs, beaten
1 tablespoon Homemade Miso (page 10), or white miso
Green part of a scallion, finely sliced

1. Heat the vegetable oil in a frying pan over medium heat. Mix the egg and miso together, pour into the pan and stir until softly scrambled. Transfer to serving plates and garnish with the scallion.

Tofu with Miso Sauce

This is a perfect choice for when you want one more dish for dinner. It's also great on its own as a snack to enjoy with drinks.

SERVES 2

Green part of a scallion, thinly sliced
1½ tablespoons Homemade Miso (page 10), or white miso
1 block atsu-age deep-fried tofu, about 5½ oz (150 g)

1. Mix the scallion and miso together. Spread on top of the block of atsu-age tofu and place the tofu on a baking sheet lined with aluminum foil. Bake in the toaster oven or in a regular oven for 7–8 minutes at about 400°F (200°C). Cut into bite-size pieces and serve.

Eggplant Wrapped in Miso Pork

Tender, melting eggplant, the rich flavor of pork belly, and the sweet, savory depth of miso—an exquisite trio in perfect harmony.

SERVES 2

2 Asian eggplants
4 tablespoons Homemade Miso (page 10), or white miso
8 slices thinly sliced pork belly
1 teaspoon vegetable oil
Radish sprouts or other microgreens, for garnish

1. Quarter each eggplant lengthwise. Spread miso on one side of each pork slice, and wrap 1 slice around each piece of eggplant, with the miso side facing the eggplant.
2. Heat the vegetable oil in a frying pan over medium heat. Put the rolls seam-side down and cook for about 1 minute to seal. Continue cooking, turning occasionally to brown all sides evenly, about 2–3 more minutes.
3. Add 2 tablespoons of water and cover with a lid. Steam-fry over low heat for 7–8 minutes. Serve garnished with the radish sprouts.

NOTE: Wrap the meat around the eggplant at a slight diagonal, overlapping a little as you go, so that the entire surface is covered and the miso flavor is distributed evenly.

Chicken Spring Rolls with Miso

Even mild-tasting chicken tenders become full of flavor with miso. These are delicious just as they are—no need for any dipping sauce! Enjoy them freshly fried.

MAKES 6 SPRING ROLLS

- 3 chicken tenders
- 3 slices processed cheese
- 2 tablespoons Homemade Miso (page 10), or white miso
- 6 spring roll wrappers
- 6 green shiso leaves
- A little flour
- Vegetable oil, for frying

1. Remove the sinews from the chicken and cut each tender in half. Cut each cheese slice in half.
2. Spread the miso evenly over one side of each chicken tender. Lay out a spring roll wrapper, and place cheese, chicken tender, and shiso leaf on top (see below). Roll it up, and seal the edge with a paste made by mixing equal parts flour and water. Repeat to make 6 spring rolls.
3. Pour about ½ inch (1.5 cm) of oil into a frying pan, and heat to 340°F (170°C). Put the spring rolls in the oil seam-side down, and deep-fry for about 3 minutes. Turn over and fry for another 3 minutes.

NOTE: Place one corner of the spring roll wrapper near you. Place a piece of cheese and then a piece of chicken on the near side, and a shiso leaf on the far side, for a neat-looking spring roll.

Miso for Main Dishes

Give your everyday meals a fresh twist with Homemade Miso. It's great for marinades and adds rich flavor to both Japanese and Western-style dishes. Lower in salt so you can use more of it, this miso brings deep umami to every bite.

Chicken Karaage with Miso

Chicken breast can be dry, but when cooked with miso, it always turns out juicy and tender, with just the right balance of saltiness and sweetness.

SERVES 2

1 lb 2 oz (500 g) boneless chicken breast
2 tablespoons cake flour
4 tablespoons potato starch or cornstarch
Vegetable oil, for frying

A Ingredients
4 tablespoons Overnight Miso, or white miso
2 teaspoons soy sauce
2 teaspoons mirin
2 teaspoons sake
1 piece ginger, grated

1. Cut the chicken into bite-size pieces.
2. Put the A ingredients in a resealable plastic bag, mix, then add the chicken and massage to coat. Remove the air from the bag, close the top, and leave in the refrigerator overnight.
3. Add the flour to the plastic bag and knead, then transfer the chicken pieces to a plate. Dust each chicken piece with the starch.
4. Heat the frying oil to 340°F (170°C), add the chicken,* and deep-fry for 3–4 minutes. Remove and let rest for 3 minutes. Heat the frying oil to 375°F (190°C) and deep-fry again for 30 seconds to 1 minute before serving.

*If you put too many pieces of chicken into the oil at once, the temperature of the oil will drop, so you may need to fry the chicken pieces in batches.

NOTE: Massage the seasoning thoroughly into the chicken so it absorbs well. Because Homemade Miso has less salt, it doesn't draw moisture out of the meat as strongly, and the flavor takes longer to work its way in. Letting it sit overnight gives the seasoning enough time to fully penetrate, resulting in juicy, flavorful chicken.

Delicious Everyday Dishes

Stir-fried Pork with Miso

A simple stir-fry of pork and bok choy gets a flavorful twist with miso and fragrant sesame oil. Finish with a dash of shichimi togarashi seven-spice blend for a little heat.

SERVES 2

2 heads baby bok choy
2 teaspoons sesame oil
7 oz (200 g) roughly chopped pork, such as for a stir-fry
Shichimi togarashi, to taste

A Ingredients (mix together)
2 tablespoons Homemade Miso (page 10), or white miso
2 tablespoons sake
1 teaspoon soy sauce

1. Cut the leafy part of each bok choy into quarters. Cut the base of each bok choy into six wedges.
2. Heat the sesame oil in a frying pan over medium heat, and stir-fry the pork and the base sections of the bok choy. When the color of the meat changes, add the rest of the bok choy and stir-fry briefly.
3. Add the A ingredients, stir-fry briefly, and sprinkle with shichimi togarashi before serving.

Miso Chicken Patties

The addition of miso gives these patties a rich flavor and a soft texture. These are great to pack into a lunchtime bento box.

SERVES 2

- 7 oz (200 g) ground chicken
- 4 inch (10 cm) piece of leek or fat green onion, minced
- 3 tablespoons Homemade Miso (page 10), or white miso
- Black pepper, to taste
- 2 teaspoons vegetable oil
- 1 tablespoon sake
- Radish sprouts or other microgreens, for garnish

1. Put the ground chicken, leek, miso and black pepper in a bowl. Moisten your hands with a little vegetable oil, and mix the ingredients together well with your hands until the meat is sticky.

2. Heat the 2 tablespoons of oil in a frying pan over medium-low heat. Put in the Step 1 patties and pan-fry for 1–2 minutes per side. Sprinkle with the sake, cover with a lid, and steam-fry for 2–3 minutes. Serve garnished with the radish sprouts.

Sea Bream with Miso and Butter

The mild flavor of the sea bream goes well with the miso and butter. The aroma of sudachi citrus or lemon is a nice accent. I also recommend making this with salmon, cod or other fish.

SERVES 2

- ½ leek or fat green onion, sliced thinly diagonally
- 2 pieces sea bream, total 5 oz (160 g)
- 2 tablespoons Homemade Miso (page 10), or white miso
- 1 tablespoon sake
- 8 cherry tomatoes
- 1 heaping tablespoon butter
- 2 slices sudachi citrus or lemon

1. Spread out a piece of aluminum foil and place half the leek and one slice of sea bream on top. Mix together the miso and sake. Spread half of the mixture over the sea bream, and place four cherry tomatoes on top. Close the foil up. Repeat with the second piece of sea bream.
2. Pour water into a frying pan to a depth of ½ inch (1 cm), bring to a boil, and arrange the two foil packets in the pan. Turn the heat to medium-low, cover with a lid, and steam-fry for about 12 minutes. Transfer to serving plates, top with butter, and garnish with sudachi citrus or lemon.

Chicken in Sesame Miso

Mild miso flavor pairs perfectly with plenty of nutty sesame. The rich, toasty aroma fills each bite—making this a warming, deeply satisfying dish.

SERVES 2

9 oz (250 g) boneless chicken thigh
2 Asian turnips, with greens
1 tablespoon sesame paste
1 tablespoon ground white sesame seeds

A Ingredients

⅔ cup (150 ml) dashi stock
2 tablespoons Homemade Miso (page 10), or white miso
2 teaspoons mirin
1 teaspoon soy sauce

1. Cut the chicken into bite-size pieces. Cut the greens of 1 turnip into 1½ inch (4 cm) pieces. (Reserve the greens of the second turnip for another use.) Peel the turnips and cut each into 6 pieces.

2. Combine the A ingredients in a pot, add the chicken, and turn the heat to medium. When the pot comes to a boil, turn the chicken over, add the turnip, and put a lid on. Turn the heat to low and simmer for about 8 minutes, stirring occasionally.

3. Add the turnip greens. Simmer for about 2 minutes, then add the sesame paste and ground sesame and mix well.

Cabbage and Pork Hot Pot with Miso

Slow-simmered napa cabbage turns meltingly tender and comforting. The mildly sweet miso broth gets a bright, zesty kick from yuzu kosho citrus-chili paste.

SERVES 2

¼ napa cabbage, about 1 lb 2 oz (500 g)
2½ cups (600 ml) dashi stock
1 leek or fat green onion, sliced thinly diagonally
1 teaspoon yuzu kosho
7 oz (200 g) pork loin, thinly sliced for shabu-shabu
Sesame oil, for drizzling

A Ingredients

4 tablespoons Homemade Miso (page 10), or white miso
1 teaspoon soy sauce
1 teaspoon sake

1. Separate the cabbage leaves from the white stems, and cut both leaves and stems into 1½ inch (4 cm) pieces.

2. Bring the dashi stock to a boil in a pot over medium heat, add the napa cabbage stems, turn the heat to medium-low and simmer, covered, for about 5 minutes.

3. Add the A ingredients, the napa cabbage leaves and the leek, and simmer for 3 minutes. Add the yuzu kosho and the pork, and when the color of the pork changes, drizzle in some sesame oil and serve.

NOTE: Dissolve the miso gradually in the hot broth as you add it to the pot.

Miso-flavored Gyoza Dumplings

The gyoza filling is flavored with miso, so these are delicious even without any dipping sauce. The shiso adds a delicate herbal note, balancing the rich taste with a clean, refreshing finish.

SERVES 2

2 cabbage leaves, about 3½ oz (100 g) total
¼ teaspoon salt
3 oz (80 g) ground pork
5 green shiso leaves, minced
12 large gyoza wrappers
1 tablespoon vegetable oil
Sesame oil, for drizzling

A Ingredients
Small piece ginger, minced
½ garlic clove, minced
1½ tablespoons Homemade Miso (page 10), or white miso
1 teaspoon sesame oil

1. Discard the core of the cabbage leaves and dice the leaves finely into ¼ inch (5 mm) pieces. Put the diced cabbage in a bowl, sprinkle with the salt, leave for 5 minutes, then squeeze out the moisture. In a separate bowl, knead the ground pork and the A ingredients together, then add the cabbage and shiso leaves and mix. Divide the mixture equally between the gyoza wrappers and fold them closed (see picture below).
2. Heat the vegetable oil in a frying pan over medium heat, turn off the heat, and arrange the gyoza dumplings in the pan. Turn the heat back on to medium, and cook for 4–5 minutes until the dumplings are browned on the bottom. Add 6½ tablespoons of water, cover the pan with a lid, and steam-cook for about 4 minutes.
3. Take the lid off. When there is almost no moisture left in the pan, drizzle in a little sesame oil, and continue cooking the gyoza dumplings until they are crispy on the bottom.

NOTE: Put about a tablespoon of filling in the center of a gyoza wrapper, wet the edges, and fold the skin over, gathering the folds in 4 or 5 places. Press the edges firmly together so that they don't come apart.

Broccoli and Bacon Miso Gratin

Homemade Miso pairs beautifully with dairy. In this recipe, its mellow, savory flavor adds depth to a creamy white sauce that makes the vegetables truly shine.

SERVES 2

½ small head of broccoli, about 5½ oz (150 g)
½ onion
2 slices bacon
1 heaping tablespoon butter
3 tablespoons cake flour
1¾ cups (400 ml) milk
3 tablespoons Homemade Miso (page 10), or white miso
Black pepper, to taste
½ cup (50 g) pizza cheese

1. Divide the broccoli into florets; discard the stem. Slice the onion thinly. Cut the bacon into ½ inch (1 cm) dice.
2. Heat the butter in a frying pan over medium heat, and stir-fry the onions and bacon until soft. Turn the heat to low, sprinkle in the flour, and cook until the flour is well blended.
3. Add the milk a little at a time, stirring constantly. Once smooth, add the broccoli, return to medium heat, and simmer until thickened. Add the miso and the black pepper and stir until the miso is well combined. Put into an oven-safe dish, sprinkle with cheese, and bake in a toaster oven for 5–8 minutes, or in a regular oven at 425°F (220°C) for about 10 minutes, until browned on top.

Chunky Vegetable Miso Stew

This hearty one-pot dish is packed with vegetables and simmered in a light miso broth that draws out the natural flavors of the ingredients.

SERVES 2

½ carrot
¼ cabbage, about 10 oz (300 g)
1 celery stalk
1 teaspoon Western-style stock granules
1 bay leaf
4 hot dogs
4 tablespoons canned kidney beans
3 tablespoons Homemade Miso (page 10), or white miso
Black pepper, for sprinkling
French mustard, to serve

1. Cut the carrot in half lengthwise. Cut the cabbage into 2 wedges. Remove the strings from the celery and cut into 3 inch (7–8 cm) pieces.

2. Put 2½ cups (600 ml) of water, the carrot and the stock granules in a heavy pot, cover with a lid and bring to a boil over medium heat. Add the bay leaf, cabbage and celery, and when it comes to a boil again, turn the heat to low and simmer, covered, for about 20 minutes.

3. When the carrot is tender add the hot dogs and kidney beans, and simmer for about 5 minutes. Mix in the miso that has been dissolved in a little of the broth, and sprinkle with black pepper. Serve in bowls with French mustard on the side.

Miso Bulgogi with Ginger

A Korean-style stir-fry of thinly sliced beef, this version is marinated in miso and plenty of fresh ginger for rich flavor and tenderness. The ginger will warm you up from the inside out.

SERVES 2

7 oz (200 g) thinly sliced beef, such as for a stir-fry
½ onion, sliced thinly lengthwise
½ red bell pepper, sliced thinly lengthwise
Cilantro, chopped, for garnish
Roasted white sesame seeds, to taste

A Ingredients
1 inch (2.5 cm) piece ginger, grated
3 tablespoons Homemade Miso (page 10), or white miso
2 tablespoons sake
2 tablespoons water
1 tablespoon sesame oil
2 teaspoons soy sauce

1. Combine the A ingredients in a bowl, add the beef, onion and bell pepper, and mix. Let it sit for about 10 minutes.

2. Transfer everything, including the marinade liquid, into a frying pan, and cook over a medium-low heat, stirring until the beef has changed color. Serve garnished with cilantro and sesame seeds.

NOTE: By marinating the ingredients in the seasoning, the flavor will soak in well, and the enzymes in the miso and onions will tenderize the meat.

Noodle and Rice Dishes

Miso blends really well with noodles and rice, and when combined with other flavoring ingredients adds a gentle richness to both Western and Japanese dishes, satisfying body and soul.

Miso Carbonara

The sauce comes together with just a quick mix in a bowl. The miso makes this dish rich and full of flavor—without using any cream.

SERVES 2

2 teaspoons salt
6½ oz (180 g) uncooked spaghetti
2 slices bacon
Coarsely ground black pepper, to serve

A Ingredients
2 eggs, room temperature
2 tablespoons Parmesan cheese
2 tablespoons Homemade Miso (page 10), or white miso

1. Bring 8¼ cups (2 L) of water to a boil in a pot, add 2 teaspoons of salt, and cook the spaghetti for the time indicated on the packet.

2. Cut the bacon into ½ inch (1 cm) dice. Put the A ingredients in a large bowl, mix well, add the bacon and mix again briefly. Add the hot, drained spaghetti and mix briefly to coat evenly. Serve sprinkled with black pepper.

NOTE: The mixture containing raw egg is added to the hot pasta, which lightly cooks the egg through residual heat—just like in classic carbonara. Use pasteurized or very fresh eggs.

Delicious Everyday Dishes

Miso Hayashi Rice

Hayashi rice is a popular Japanese comfort food made with beef and onion in a tomato sauce, typically served over rice. This version adds miso for a uniquely savory twist. It also works well with Black Soybean Miso (page 15).

SERVES 2

2 tablespoons olive oil
1 onion, halved lengthwise, then cut into ½ inch (1 cm) slices
5½ oz (150 g) thinly sliced beef, such as for a stir-fry
5½ oz (150 g) button mushrooms, sliced thinly
Salt and pepper, for seasoning
1 tablespoon cake flour
3½ tablespoons red wine
½ small can whole tomatoes, 7 oz (200 g), crushed
2 servings warm cooked medium-grain Japonica rice
Chopped parsley, to serve

A ingredients (mix together)
4 tablespoons Overnight Miso, or white miso
1 tablespoon Japanese Worcestershire sauce
1 tablespoon tomato ketchup

1. Heat the olive oil in a frying pan over medium heat, and stir-fry the onion until soft. Add the beef and mushrooms, season with salt and pepper, and stir-fry until the beef changes color. Sprinkle in the flour and stir-fry until the flouriness is gone.

2. Add the red wine and bring to a boil. Add the tomatoes and 6½ tablespoons water. Cover and bring back to a boil, then lower the heat and simmer for about 10 minutes, stirring occasionally. Add the combined A ingredients and bring to a boil. Serve with rice and sprinkle with parsley.

Miso Butter Chicken Curry

This classic curry dish takes on a whole new dimension with the addition of miso, which softens the acidity and spiciness to just the right degree, resulting in a rich, well-rounded and irresistible flavor.

SERVES 2

9 oz (250 g) boneless chicken thigh, cut into bite-size pieces
¼ teaspoon salt
Pinch of black pepper
2 tablespoons vegetable oil
1 onion, minced
5 green beans, each cut into 4 pieces
3 tablespoons Homemade Miso (page 10), or white miso
1 heaping tablespoon butter
2 servings warm cooked mixed grain rice
Plain yogurt, to taste

A Ingredients
3 tablespoons plain yogurt
2 tablespoons curry powder

B ingredients
½ small can whole tomatoes, 7 oz (200 g), crushed
1 piece ginger, grated
1 garlic clove, grated

1. Sprinkle the chicken pieces with the salt and pepper, and put in a resealable plastic bag. Add the A ingredients and massage to coat the chicken evenly. Remove the air from the bag, seal it and refrigerate overnight.
2. Heat the oil in a frying pan over medium heat, and brown the onion. Move the onion to the side, add the chicken and marinade, and fry for 2–3 minutes on each side. Add the B ingredients and stir-fry for 3-4 minutes. Add 6½ tablespoons of water and bring to a boil. Turn the heat to medium-low, cover, and simmer for 8 minutes, stirring occasionally.
3. Add the green beans and cook, stirring, for 2 minutes. Add the miso and butter, and mix well. Serve over the rice, topped with yogurt.

NOTE: By massaging the yogurt and curry powder into the chicken and letting it sit overnight, the meat becomes tender and develops a rich flavor.

Miso Soy Milk Tantanmen

This dish of Japanese-style dan dan noodles in a light, creamy miso broth is easy on the palate. With both miso and soy milk, you get a double dose of the goodness of soy.

SERVES 2

1 teaspoon sesame oil
3½ oz (100 g) ground pork
½ teaspoon doubanjiang
1 teaspoon oyster sauce
1 teaspoon Homemade Miso (page 10), or white miso
½ teaspoon chicken stock granules
2 servings Chinese noodles, about 4 oz (120 g) each
Cilantro, roughly chopped, for garnish

A Ingredients
4 inch (10 cm) piece leek or fat green onion, minced
Small piece ginger, minced
½ garlic clove, minced

B ingredients (mix together)
¾ cup (200 ml) unsweetened soy milk
3 tablespoons Homemade Miso (page 10), or white miso
1 tablespoon white roasted sesame seeds
1 teaspoon soy sauce

1. Heat the sesame oil and the A ingredients in a frying pan over medium heat until fragrant. Add the pork and doubanjiang and stir-fry. When the meat changes color, add the oyster sauce and the 1 teaspoon of miso and stir to combine. Take out the contents of the frying pan and set aside.
2. Clean out the Step 1 frying pan. Put in ¾ cup (200 ml) water and the chicken stock granules. Bring to a boil over medium heat. Mix in the B ingredients.
3. In a separate pan, cook the noodles following the packet instructions and rinse them under running water. Drain well and arrange on plates. Pour the Step 2 sauce over the noodles and served topped with the cooked pork and the cilantro.

Chilled Udon Noodles with Chicken

Served with a soy milk sauce that brings out the flavor of the miso. The mashed umeboshi plum adds a delicious tang.

SERVES 2

4 chicken tenders, about 8 oz (220 g) total
1 tablespoon sake
Salt, for sprinkling
2 servings frozen udon noodles, about 4 oz (120 g) each
1 Japanese or Asian cucumber, julienned
2 umeboshi plums, pitted and mashed

A ingredients (mix together)
⅔ cup (150 ml) unsweetened soy milk
2½ tablespoons Homemade Miso (page 10), or white miso
2 tablespoons ground white sesame seeds
2 teaspoons light or regular soy sauce

1. Place the chicken tenders on a microwave-safe plate, sprinkle with the sake and salt, and cover loosely with plastic wrap. Microwave on medium for about 2 minutes 30 seconds until just cooked through (see note below). Leave to cool slightly in the plastic wrap, then shred into easy-to-eat pieces.
2. Cook the udon noodles following the packet instructions. Rinse under cold running water, drain well and arrange in individual serving bowls. Top with the cucumber and Step 1 chicken, pour on the combined A ingredients, and serve with the umeboshi on the side.

NOTE: Microwave cooking times given in this book are based on a 600W microwave. If using a 500W model, increase the time by approximately 1.2 times. Cooking times may vary slightly depending on the appliance.

Chicken and Lotus Root Rice with Miso

A delicious rice dish filled with the savory flavor of chicken and the rich depth of miso. By soaking the rice thoroughly, it cooks up perfectly even with toppings added.

SERVES 4–5

1½ cups (300 g) uncooked medium-grain Japonica rice, rinsed and soaked in water for 30 minutes, then drained
5½ oz (150 g) lotus root, cut into ½ inch (1 cm) cubes and soaked in water for 5 minutes
5½ oz (150 g) boneless chicken thigh, cut into ½ inch (1.5 cm) cubes
Green part of scallion, chopped, for garnish

A ingredients (mix together)
4 tablespoons Homemade Miso (page 10), or white miso
2 tablespoons sake
4 teaspoons soy sauce

1. Put the rice and combined A ingredients into a rice cooker, add water up to the 2-cup mark, and mix lightly. Place the drained lotus root and chicken on top and cook.
2. Mix lightly, and serve garnished with the scallion.

Fried Rice with Miso and Pickles

The gentle sweetness of the miso and the salty tang of the pickled takana greens are a perfect match. The crunchy texture of the pine nuts adds a nice accent.

SERVES 2

2 servings warm cooked medium-grain Japonica rice
2 tablespoons sesame oil
2½ oz (70 g) takana mustard greens, roughly chopped
4 inch (10 cm) piece leek or fat green onion, minced
1 tablespoon pine nuts

A Ingredients
1 egg
2 tablespoons Homemade Miso (page 10), or white miso
1 teaspoon soy sauce
A little red chili pepper, minced, to taste

1. Put the A ingredients in a bowl and mix. Add the rice and mix again.
2. Heat the sesame oil in a frying pan over medium-high heat, add the rice and stir-fry, breaking up any clumps. When the grains are loose and separated, add the takana and stir-fry together. Add the leek and pine nuts and stir-fry briefly before serving.

NOTE: By coating the rice with the egg mixture beforehand, the flavor spreads evenly and the final dish turns out light and fluffy.

Pickles and Marinades Using Miso

Just mix four parts miso and one part mirin to make a delicious marinade for meat and fish. Since it burns easily, adjust the heat as needed while cooking. Any miso scraped off the surface of the meat or fish before cooking can be reused in miso soup — just be sure to heat it thoroughly!

Pan-fried Pork Marinated in Miso

The sweet miso flavor soaks in slowly, blending with the richness of the pork fat for an irresistible flavor.

SERVES 2

- 2 pork shoulder fillets, about 10 oz (300 g) total
- 4 tablespoons Homemade Miso (page 10), or white miso
- 1 tablespoon mirin
- 2 teaspoons sesame oil
- 2–3 lettuce leaves, shredded

1. Score the pork fillets to prevent curling and place in a resealable plastic bag. Mix the miso and mirin together and add to the bag. Massage the bag to coat the pork all over with the marinade. Remove the air, close the bag, and leave it in the refrigerator overnight.

2. Heat the sesame oil in a frying pan over medium-low heat. Remove the pork from the bag, wipe off excess marinade with a rubber spatula, and add the pork to the pan. Cook for 2–3 minutes, flip, and reduce the heat to low. Cover the pan with a lid and cook for another 3–4 minutes. Slice each fillet and serve with the lettuce on the side.

NOTE: Put the pork and miso–mirin marinade into a resealable plastic bag and massage the bag to coat the pork. Rubbing in the marinade well will help the flavors to penetrate and make the meat tender.

Delicious Everyday Dishes

Grilled Salmon Marinated in Miso

This has a milder flavor than plain salt-grilled fish—it's perfect for bento box lunches too. You can use this marinade with other fish, like yellowtail or sea bream.

SERVES 2

8 shishito peppers
2 pieces fresh salmon, about 7 oz (200 g) total
4 tablespoons Homemade Miso (page 10), or white miso
1 tablespoon mirin

1. Poke several holes in each shishito pepper with a wooden skewer.
2. Put the salmon in a resealable plastic bag. Mix the miso and mirin together and add to the bag. Massage the bag gently so that the fish is thoroughly coated. Remove the air from the bag, seal it, and leave in the refrigerator overnight.
3. Remove the salmon from the bag, scrape off the marinade with a rubber spatula, and arrange the salmon on a grill rack. Add the shishito peppers alongside, and grill for about 5–6 minutes.

Cucumber and Turnip Miso Pickles

Miso is also great for pickling vegetables! Since Homemade Miso is low in salt, there's no need to wipe it off the pickles before eating—just enjoy as is!

SERVES 2

4 tablespoons Homemade Miso (page 10), or white miso
1 tablespoon mirin, brought to a boil*
1 Japanese or Asian cucumber, sliced thinly diagonally
1 Asian turnip, 3½ oz (100 g), cut in half lengthwise then sliced thinly lengthwise

*Put into a microwave-safe container uncovered, and microwave for 40–50 seconds to boil off the alcohol (see note, page 59).

1. Put the miso and mirin in a resealable plastic bag and rub the bag to combine. Add the cucumber and turnip, massage the bag to coat them well, and refrigerate overnight.

Everyday Sides

These simple make-ahead dishes are great as sides or as accompaniments to rice. Simple everyday ingredients take on a fresh twist when seasoned with Homemade Miso.

Carrot with Walnuts

Miso adds sweetness and walnuts add crunch. Keeps for 3–4 days in the refrigerator.

AN EASY TO MAKE AMOUNT

1 teaspoon olive oil
1 carrot, shredded
Handful roasted walnuts, about 1 oz (30 g)

A Ingredients (mix together)
2 tablespoons Homemade Miso (page 10), or white miso
2 teaspoons mirin
2 teaspoons rice vinegar
2 teaspoons water

1. Heat the olive oil in a frying pan over medium heat, and stir-fry the carrot. Once the carrot is coated with the oil add the A ingredients, and stir well to combine. Coarsely chop the walnuts and mix in.

Chicken with Lotus Root

Great on its own or mixed into omelets. Keeps for 4–5 days in the refrigerator.

AN EASY TO MAKE AMOUNT

7 oz (200 g) ground chicken
2½ oz (70 g) lotus root, cut in ¼ inch (5 mm) dice

A Ingredients (mix together)
3 tablespoons Homemade Miso (page 10), or white miso
2 tablespoons sake
2 tablespoons water
1 tablespoon soy sauce
1 tablespoon mirin

1. Put all the ingredients into a pot, and cook over medium heat. Stir until most of the liquid has evaporated and the ingredients are lightly browned.

Miso Kinpira

Kinpira is a traditional dish of sautéed vegetables. Keeps for 4–5 days in the refrigerator.

AN EASY TO MAKE AMOUNT

1 burdock root, about 5½ oz (150 g)
1 teaspoon sesame oil
1 small red chili pepper, thinly sliced
¼ carrot, cut into thin strips
Roasted white sesame seeds, for garnish

A ingredients (mix together)
2 tablespoons Homemade Miso (page 10), or white miso
1 tablespoon mirin
1 tablespoon sake
1 tablespoon water
1 teaspoon soy sauce

1. Peel and thinly shave the burdock root and soak in a bowl of water for 5 minutes.
2. Heat the sesame oil in a frying pan over medium heat, and fry the chili pepper, drained burdock root and carrot for 2–3 minutes. When the burdock root has become transparent, add the A ingredients and stir-fry until the liquid has evaporated. Serve sprinkled with the sesame seeds.

Greens with Miso and Tofu

Enjoy the natural sweetness of the greens. Keeps for 1–2 days in the refrigerator.

AN EASY TO MAKE AMOUNT

½ block silken tofu, about 7 oz (200 g)
Pinch of salt
Bunch of spinach, about 7 oz (200 g)
Small bunch chrysanthemum greens, about 3½ oz (100 g)

A Ingredients
3 tablespoons Homemade Miso, or white miso
3 tablespoons ground white sesame seeds

1. Wrap the tofu in two layers of paper towels and place on a microwave-safe plate. Microwave for 1 minute 30 seconds, and let cool for 15 minutes (see note, page 59).
2. Boil some water in a pot, add a pinch of salt, and hold the stems of the spinach and chrysanthemum greens in the water. After about 30 seconds, submerge the entire bunch and boil for another 10 seconds. Cool in cold water, squeeze out the water well, and cut into 1½ inch (4 cm) pieces.
3. Put the tofu and A ingredients into a bowl and mix well until smooth. Add the greens and mix.

Cucumber with Vinegar Miso

The crisp, refreshing texture, with a subtle kick of mustard, will have you coming back for more. Keeps for 3–4 days in the refrigerator.

AN EASY TO MAKE AMOUNT

2 pinches salt
2 Japanese or Asian cucumbers, sliced thinly

A ingredients (mix together)
2 tablespoons Homemade Miso (page 10), or white miso
1 tablespoon mirin, brought to a boil*
1 teaspoon rice vinegar
¼ teaspoon Japanese karashi mustard

1. Sprinkle salt over the cucumbers, leave for 5 minutes, then squeeze out the moisture.
2. Add the A ingredients and mix.

*Put into a microwave-safe container uncovered, and microwave for 40–50 seconds to boil off the alcohol. (See note, page 59.)

Korean-style Miso Bell Pepper Namul

This dish is seasoned and cooked in the Korean *namul* style, using sesame oil. Keeps for 2–3 days in the refrigerator.

AN EASY TO MAKE AMOUNT

1 yellow bell pepper
2 teaspoons sesame oil
1 teaspoon roasted white sesame seeds

A Ingredients (mix together)
1 tablespoon Homemade Miso (page 10), or white miso
1 tablespoon water
1 teaspoon soy sauce

1. Halve the pepper lengthwise. Remove the seeds. Cut each half crosswise into ½ inch (1 cm) strips.
2. Heat the sesame oil in a frying pan over medium heat, and briefly stir-fry the pepper. Add the A ingredients and continue to cook until most of the liquid has evaporated. Sprinkle with the sesame seeds, mix and serve.

Miso Potatoes

These are good when cold too, so they work well as a snack or an appetizer to go with drinks. Keeps for 2–3 days in the refrigerator.

AN EASY TO MAKE AMOUNT

4 small potatoes, about 14 oz (400 g) total
2 tablespoons olive oil
Ground red chili pepper, to serve

A ingredients (mix together)
3 tablespoons Homemade Miso (page 10), or white miso
1 tablespoon mirin
1 tablespoon sake
½ garlic clove, grated

1. Cut each potato into about 6 pieces. Put the potato pieces on a microwave-safe plate, cover loosely with plastic wrap, and cook in the microwave for about 6 minutes (see note on page 59) until a wooden skewer can be easily inserted into the potato.
2. Heat the olive oil in a frying pan over medium heat, add the potato pieces, and cook until browned. Turn the heat to low, add the A ingredients, and stir-fry until the liquid evaporates. Serve sprinkled with ground red chili pepper.

Daikon Stewed in Miso

Dried, shredded daikon radish, called kiriboshi daikon goes well with miso. This dish keeps for 3–4 days in the refrigerator.

AN EASY TO MAKE AMOUNT

2 oz (60 g) kiriboshi daikon
2 tablespoons vegetable oil
¼ carrot, cut into thin strips
1 piece abura-age deep-fried tofu skin; halve lengthwise and cut into ½ inch (1 cm) strips

A ingredients (mix together)
1½ cups (300 ml) dashi stock
3 tablespoons Homemade Miso, or white miso
2 tablespoon mirin
1 tablespoon soy sauce

1. Rinse the kiriboshi daikon and rehydrate in water to cover for about 20 minutes.
2. Heat the oil in a pot over medium heat, and stir-fry the kiriboshi daikon, which has been squeezed to remove the water, for 1 minute. Add the carrot and tofu, fry briefly, then add the A ingredients.
3. When the pot comes to a boil, put a small lid that fits inside the pot directly on top of the contents of the pot. Simmer on low for 20 minutes.

Dressings

These dressings really enhance the flavors of ingredients — plus, they have health benefits, for a win-win! Use them for salads, for seasoning stir-fries and as dipping sauces. The recipes on this page each yield about ⅔ cup (150 ml) and keep in the refrigerator for 3–4 days.

Miso Dressing

Even a simple salad of lettuce leaves will disappear in no time with this dressing. Pour it on generously!

1. Mix together 3 tablespoons each of Homemade Miso or white miso, olive oil, and water, with 1½ tablespoons of rice vinegar.

Umeboshi Miso Dressing

The tartness of umeboshi pickled plum adds a refreshing touch. This is also great as an accompaniment to pork shabu-shabu.

1. Mix together 3 tablespoons each of Homemade Miso or white miso, olive oil and water, with the chopped up flesh of 3 umeboshi plums, plus 1 tablespoon of rice vinegar.

Onion Miso Dressing

Onion adds a natural boost for heart-healthy circulation.

1. Microwave half a grated onion for 1 minute 30 seconds (see note, page 59). Mix with 2 tablespoons each of Homemade Miso or white miso, soy sauce, olive oil and rice vinegar.

Chinese Ginger Dressing

Perfect for flavoring stir-fries and steamed dishes too.

1. Mix together 2 teaspoons of grated fresh ginger; 2 tablespoons each of Homemade Miso or white miso, sesame oil and rice vinegar; plus 4 teaspoons of soy sauce.

From left to right: Miso Dressing, Umeboshi Miso Dressing, Onion Miso Dressing and Chinese Ginger Dressing.

Sauces

Discover delicious new flavors by adding savory, sour or spicy seasonings to Homemade Miso. These sauces are great for drizzling, for tossing, or as dips. The recipes on this page each yield about 3½ tablespoons and keep in the refrigerator for 3–4 days.

Sesame Miso Sauce

A versatile sauce that can be used in a wide range of dishes, such as salads and steamed chicken.

1. Mix together 2 tablespoons of Homemade Miso or white miso, 1 tablespoon of mirin (brought to a boil*), 1 tablespoon of water, 2 teaspoons of ground white sesame seeds, and 1 teaspoon of rice vinegar.

* Put into a microwave-safe container uncovered, and microwave for 40–50 seconds to boil off the alcohol (see note, page 59).

Gochujang Miso Sauce

A spicy hot sauce that goes well with warm vegetables, hot tofu, steamed chicken or gyoza dumplings.

1. Mix together 1 tablespoon of Homemade Miso or white miso, 1 tablespoon of mirin (brought to a boil, see previous recipe), 2 teaspoons of gochujang Korean chili paste (see homemade recipe on page 86), and 1 teaspoon of rice vinegar.

Miso Sauce with Onion

The onion gives this sauce a satisfying texture. Goes well with deep-fried foods like karaage.

1. Finely mince a 2 inch (5 cm) piece of the white part of a leek or fat green onion. Combine with 2 tablespoons of Homemade Miso or white miso, and 1 tablespoon each of black vinegar, sesame oil and water.

Dips

Thanks to its lower salt content, Homemade Miso makes a great ready-to-eat dip. Pair it with raw vegetables, bread, or crackers and serve for snacking, entertaining, or with drinks. The recipes below keep for 3–4 days in the refrigerator.

Walnut and Miso Dip

Add a nutty fragrance to the mellow flavor of miso.

SERVES 2–3

1. Coarsely chop ¾ oz (20 g) of roasted walnuts. Mix with 4 tablespoons of Homemade Miso or white miso.

Cheesy Miso Dip

Cheese and miso go well together. Vegetables are delicious with this dip!

SERVES 2–3

1. Mix together 2 tablespoons of Homemade Miso or white miso, and 2 tablespoons of cream cheese.

72   The Miso Cookbook

Sweet Treats with Miso

The gentle sweetness and mild saltiness of Homemade Miso make it perfect for desserts, too. From stir-and-freeze miso ice cream that you can whip up on the spot, to banana bread that's great for breakfast, these sweet-and-savory treats are wholesome, satisfying and comforting.

Miso Ice Cream

Just mix it into store-bought ice cream. The sweet-salty flavor is seriously addictive. Chilling it again after mixing makes it easier to scoop and serve.

SERVES 2

1 cup + 3 tablespoons (280 ml) vanilla ice cream
3 tablespoons Homemade Miso (page 10), or white miso

1. Leave the ice cream out at room temperature for about 3 minutes. Mix together with the miso. Chill again before serving.

Kinako Miso Truffles

These bite-size chocolate truffles are given a Japanese touch with kinako roasted soybean powder. No cream is used but they're deliciously soft and rich.

MAKES ABOUT 12 TRUFFLES

3 oz (80 g) white chocolate, chopped
1 tablespoon Homemade Miso (page 10), or white miso
1 tablespoon milk, room temperature
1 tablespoon peanuts, or nuts of your choice, coarsely chopped
Kinako roasted soybean powder, for coating

1. Place the chocolate in a bowl and set it over a pan of water heated to about 122°F (50°C). Stir with a rubber spatula until melted. Remove from the heat and mix in the miso and milk until smooth. Stir in the peanuts.
2. Scoop out a bite-size spoonful at a time and drop onto a baking sheet lined with kitchen parchment paper. Chill in the refrigerator, uncovered, for about 30 minutes. Form each piece into a ball and roll each ball in the kinako until evenly coated. Chill again before serving.

NOTE: If the water feels slightly hot to the touch, it is around 122°F (50°C). Don't let the hot water get too hot, or the chocolate will separate.

Sweet Treats with Miso

Miso Sesame Cookies

These miso-flavored shortbread cookies with the nutty aroma of black sesame are a favorite in my family. You won't be able to stop eating them!

NOTE: Rubbing the mixture thoroughly by hand until crumbly is the key to achieving a crisp, tender texture.

MAKES ABOUT 28 COOKIES 1½ INCHES (3.5 CM) IN DIAMETER

1 tablespoon Homemade Miso (page 10), or white miso
3 tablespoons light sesame oil or vegetable oil
2 teaspoons unsweetened soy milk

A Ingredients
⅔ cup (75 g) cake flour
3 tablespoons almond flour
2 heaping tablespoons raw cane sugar
2 tablespoons roasted black sesame seeds
Pinch of salt

1. Put the A ingredients in a bowl and mix with a spoon. Add the miso and sesame oil and mix with your hands until the mixture is evenly crumbly. Add the soy milk and mix with your hands to bring the dough together.

2. Transfer the dough to your work surface and roll it out to about ¼ inch (5mm) thick. Cut into cookie shapes with a cookie cutter. Place on a baking sheet lined with kitchen parchment paper, and bake in a preheated oven at 340°F (170°C) for 15–20 minutes. Cool on a wire rack.

Miso Cheesecake

The subtle saltiness of the miso enhances the flavor of the cheese—perfect for those who don't really have a sweet tooth. This cheesecake also freezes well.

MAKES 1 CAKE, 6 INCHES (15 CM) IN DIAMETER

- 7 oz (200 g) cream cheese, room temperature
- 3 tablespoons Homemade Miso (page 10), or white miso
- 4 tablespoons granulated sugar
- ⅓ cup (80 ml) heavy cream
- 1 beaten egg, room temperature
- 2 tablespoons cake flour

*To freeze, cut into easy-to-eat pieces, wrap in plastic wrap and store in the freezer for up to one month. Defrost in the refrigerator before eating.

1. Put the cream cheese and miso in a bowl, and mix with a rubber spatula until smooth. Add the sugar and mix. Add the heavy cream and beaten egg little by little, and mix gently with a whisk each time.

2. Once the mixture is smooth, sift in the flour. Use the rubber spatula to gently fold from the bottom until no dry spots remain (see note below). Pour the batter into a baking dish lined with kitchen parchment paper and smooth the surface. Gently tap the baking dish on the counter a few times to release any trapped air bubbles, lifting it about 1 inch (3 cm) each time.

3. Preheated the oven to 356°F (180°C) and bake for 40–50 minutes. The cheesecake is done when a skewer inserted in the center comes out clean. Let cool to room temperature, then refrigerate overnight before serving.

NOTE: Once you add the flour, be careful not to overmix—the texture will suffer. Gently fold it in using a rubber spatula until just combined.

Sweet Treats with Miso

Miso Milk Pudding

Miso and milk go together perfectly. The salty umami of the miso adds complexity to the milk's natural sweetness.

MAKES 4 CUPS

1¾ cups (400 ml) milk
4 tablespoons raw cane sugar
3 tablespoons Homemade Miso (page 10), or white miso
1 teaspoon gelatin powder, sprinkled with 1 tablespoon water and left to swell up
⅔ cup (150 ml) heavy cream

1. Put the milk and sugar in a saucepan and heat over medium, stirring constantly, until just before it comes to a boil. Remove from the heat, and add the miso and gelatin, stirring until fully dissolve. Strain the mixture through a fine-mesh sieve into a mixing bowl.

2. Stir in the heavy cream, then pour the mixture into cups or ramekins. Chill in the refrigerator for 4–5 hours, or until set.

NOTE: Strain the miso mixture through a fine-mesh sieve to make it smooth. If any koji remains in the sieve, press it through or mash it well and stir it back in.

Ma Lai Go Sponge Cake with Miso

Ma Lai Go is a traditional Cantonese steamed sponge cake. This version uses miso for a Japanese-inspired twist—it's a great choice for breakfast!

MAKES 1 CAKE, 6 INCHES (15 CM) IN DIAMETER

A Ingredients
2 tablespoons unsweetened soy milk (room temperature)
3 tablespoons Homemade Miso (page 10), or white miso
3 tablespoons coconut oil, or vegetable oil
1 tablespoon honey

B ingredients
1 cup (120 g) cake flour
5½ tablespoons raw cane sugar
2 teaspoons baking powder

1. Put the A ingredients in a bowl, and whisk together until the mixture lightens slightly in color.
2. Combine the B ingredients and sift them into the bowl. Using a rubber spatula, gently fold from the bottom until the batter is smooth and glossy. Be careful not to overmix, as this can prevent the cake from rising properly.
3. Pour into a cake pan lined with kitchen parchment paper and steam in a steamer for about 30 minutes.

*Can also be frozen. Cut into quarters, wrap in plastic wrap and store in the freezer. Will keep for about a month. To eat, defrost at room temperature, mist with water, place on a microwave-safe dish, cover with plastic wrap and microwave (about 50 seconds for one quarter of the cake). See note about microwaving on page 59.

NOTE: If whisked together well until the mixture turns pale, the batter will be smooth and even.

Miso Banana Bread

The miso gives this banana bread a moist texture when baked. It's perfect for breakfast or as an afternoon snack.

MAKES 1 RECTANGULAR CAKE, 7 x 3½ x 2¼ INCHES (17.5 x 9 x 6 CM)

1 large banana, about 7 oz (200 g)
2 tablespoons light sesame oil, or vegetable oil

A Ingredients
2 eggs
4 tablespoons Homemade Miso (page 10), or white miso
4 tablespoons raw cane sugar

B ingredients (combined)
¾ cup (100 g) cake flour
1 teaspoon baking powder

1. Roughly mash the banana with a fork. (If it isn't fully ripe, heat it in the microwave* for about 1 minute to make it easier to mash).
2. Put the A ingredients in a bowl and mix with a hand mixer for about 2 minutes. Add the sesame oil and mix for another minute. Add the banana, mix briefly with a rubber spatula, then sift in the combined B ingredients. Mix while scooping up from the bottom of the bowl with the rubber spatula.
3. When the flouriness has disappeared, pour the batter into a loaf pan lined with kitchen parchment paper and bake in a preheated oven at 355°F (180°C) for 30–40 minutes or until a skewer inserted into the center comes out clean.

*See note, page 59.

NOTE: After baking for 10 minutes, make a slit down the center of the loaf. Rotate the pan front to back to ensure even baking. If the surface starts to brown too quickly, cover it loosely with aluminum foil.

Easy-to-Make Fermented Seasonings

Rice koji can be used to make a variety of homemade seasonings beyond miso, like shio koji (salt koji) and shoyu koji (soy sauce koji), to brighten up your everyday meals with a depth of flavor you can't get from store-bought condiments. Most are simple to make—just mix and let ferment. In this section there's also a recipe for the sweet fermented rice drink amazake.

Shio Koji

This versatile seasoning, with rich umami and just the right amount of salt, goes well with any ingredient. Use it to marinate meat or fish, and they'll turn out moist and tender. Keeps for 3 months in the refrigerator.

AN EASY TO MAKE AMOUNT

7 oz (200 g) fresh rice koji
2 oz (60 g) salt

1. Put the rice koji in a bowl and break up any clumps with your hands.

2. Add the salt and mix.

3. Add ¾ cup (200 ml) water.

*If using dried rice koji, increase the water added to 1 cup (250 ml).

4. Mix well. If the surface is still dry after mixing, add a little more water.

*The amount of water will vary depending on the humidity and the condition of the koji, so adjust it so that the water is evenly distributed.

5. Transfer to a clean enamel or glass container.

6. Cover with a lid, and leave at room temperature for 4 days to 1 week. Stir once a day with a clean spoon.

7. When the rice koji has softened, the shio koji is done.

Fermented Seasonings

Shoyu Koji

Shoyu koji (soy sauce koji) has a touch of natural sweetness. It's perfect to season salads and stir-fries, or as a dipping sauce for hot pot dishes. Keeps for 3 months in the refrigerator.

AN EASY TO MAKE AMOUNT

3½ oz (100 g) fresh rice koji
¾ cup (200 ml) soy sauce*

*Use the same amount of soy sauce for dried koji.

1. Put the koji in a clean enamel or glass container. Break up any clumps. Add the soy sauce.

2. Cover with a lid. Leave 7–10 days at room temperature. Stir once a day with a clean spoon.

3. When the rice koji has softened, the shoyu koji is done.

Fish Sauce Koji

Rice koji is mixed with umami-rich Thai fish sauce. The koji balances out the fishiness of the sauce. Use to sauté meat or fish, or for soups. Keeps for 3 months in the refrigerator.

AN EASY TO MAKE AMOUNT

1 oz (30 g) fresh rice koji
6½ tablespoons nam pla Thai fish sauce*

*Use the same amount of nam pla for dried koji.

1. Put the rice koji in a clean enamel or glass container. Break up any clumps. Add the nam pla.

2. Cover with a lid. Leave 7–10 days at room temperature. Stir once a day with a clean spoon.

3. When the rice koji has softened, the fish sauce koji is done.

Fermented Seasonings

Easy Gochujang Korean Chili Paste

This hot pepper paste has just the right amount of spiciness and sweetness. Add it to miso soup, or mix it with mayonnaise and use as a dip. Keeps for 2–3 weeks in the refrigerator.

AN EASY TO MAKE AMOUNT

2 oz (50 g) fresh rice koji
1 tablespoon gochugaru Korean chili powder, ideally a mix of coarse and fine grind
1 teaspoon salt

1. Put all the ingredients in a resealable plastic bag. (I recommend a bag, as a container may absorb color and odor.) Add ⅓ cup (80 ml) of 140°F (60°C) water.
*Use the same amount of hot water for dried rice koji.

2. Rub and knead the bag to evenly distribute the water.

3. Line the inner pot of a rice cooker with a kitchen cloth or cheesecloth and put the bag inside. Set the rice cooker to the "keep warm" setting, leaving the bag slightly open, and leave for 8–10 hours.

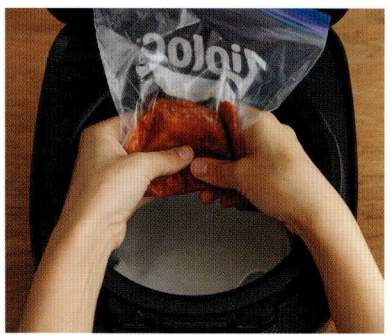

4. Every 2–3 hours, take the bag out and knead gently to mix the contents.

5. When the contents are smooth and thick, the gochujang is done. Transfer to a clean storage jar.

Amazake

Amazake is a Japanese drink traditionally made with fermented rice—this non-alcoholic version uses just rice koji. You can enjoy the grainy texture, or use a blender to make it smooth. Keeps refrigerated for up to 1 week, or frozen for up to 1 month. To freeze, place in a resealable plastic bag and flatten into a thin sheet. It won't freeze solid; you can break of pieces as needed.

AN EASY TO MAKE AMOUNT

7 oz (200 g) fresh rice koji

1. Put the rice koji and 1¾ cups (400 ml) of 140°F (60°C) water into a rice cooker pot.
*Use the same amount of hot water for dried rice koji.

2. Mix so that the water is evenly distributed.

3. Put the pot inside the rice cooker, and set to "keep warm." Leave the lid open, and cover the top with a double layer of damp cloth. Let it sit for 8–10 hours.

4. Every 2–3 hours, stir the mixture and re-dampen the cloth before covering it again. It's ready when it thickens to a smooth, pourable consistency. Transfer to a clean storage container.

Fermented Seasonings

Traditional Miso

Making miso the old-fashioned way is easier than you might think—just mix the ingredients and ferment at room temperature for six months. This slow-fermented miso has a deep, complex flavor, while Homemade Miso offers a milder, fresher taste. Each has its own unique character—try both and see which you prefer!

MAKES 3½ LBS (1.6 KG)

10 oz (300 g) dried soybeans
1 lb 4 oz (600 g) fresh rice koji
6 oz (165 g) salt

1. To prevent mold growth, spray the clean enamel or similar non-reactive container with food-grade alcohol.

2. Follow steps 1, 2 and 4 of the recipe for Homemade Miso (page 10) to cook, mash and cool the soybeans, reserving the soybean cooking water. Put the rice koji and salt in a resealable plastic bag and shake to mix.

3. Put the mashed soybeans in a large bowl. Add the koji and salt mixture in batches, mixing thoroughly with your hands, kneading and pressing it together.

4. Gradually add about ⅔ cup (150 ml) of the soybean cooking water while mixing; the mixture should be slightly moister than finished miso.

5. Take a handful of the mixture, roll it into a ball and squeeze tightly to eliminate the air.

6. Form the rest of the mixture into balls too, and stuff tightly into a container.

> Check the progression of the miso from time to time. If you see any mold, remove it along with the surrounding area, and spray the area directly with alcohol. Replace with a new piece of plastic wrap and put the lid back on.

7. Smooth out the surface of the mixture and cover with plastic wrap that is in direct contact with the surface. Cover with a lid, and leave for about six months in a room temperature location out of direct sunlight.

8. When the flavor is mild and well rounded and the color is deeper, the miso is done. Store in the refrigerator.

Fermented Seasonings

Glossary of Ingredients

abura-age tofu
Sometimes called "fried-skin tofu." This is a thin sheet of tofu that has been deep fried until golden brown. You can find abura-age at Japanese grocery stores.

adzuki beans
Small, reddish-brown legumes often used in East Asian cuisine. They have a slightly sweet, nutty flavor and a firm texture. You can find them at regular supermarkets.

aosa seaweed
Often called "sea lettuce" in English, it can be bought as dried leaves or in flaked form from Japanese grocery stores.

atsu-age tofu
is thick, firm tofu that has been deep-fried, giving it a crispy outside and soft interior. Find it at Japanese grocery stores, or regular groceries, where it might be labeled "fried tofu."

burdock root
A long, brown fibrous root vegetable with a wonderful aroma and crunchy texture. Available at Japanese, Korean and some general Asian stores.

Chinese noodles
Wheat noodles with a firm, springy texture and a yellowish color. You can find fresh (or fresh-frozen) Chinese noodles at most Chinese or Asian grocery stores.

chrysanthemum greens
Called *shungiku* in Japanese and also known garland chrysanthemum, these leafy greens have a distinctive herbal, slightly bitter flavor, adding a fragrant, peppery note to dishes. Find them in Asian grocery stores and farmers' markets.

cucumber
The cucumbers used in this book are the small, seedless Japanese or Asian variety. Find at your Asian grocery store.

daikon radish
A thick white root vegetable with a spicy flavor and a crunchy texture when raw. When cooked, it becomes soft and sweet. You can find it at Asian grocery stores as well as at many regular supermarkets.

dashi stock
Instant dashi is an easy way to make dashi stock. It typically comes as granules or powder and is just dissolved in hot water. An average measure is ½–1 teaspoon of dashi powder per 1 cup (240 ml) water. Buy at Asian grocery stores; look for labels like Hondashi (a common brand), "dashi granules" or "instant dashi stock powder."

doubanjiang
A spicy, salty Chinese fermented paste made from broad beans, chili peppers, and soybeans. Find it at Asian grocery stores.

eggplant, Asian
Smaller and thinner than the Western variety. Find them at Asian grocery stores, well-stocked supermarkets and farmers' markets.

fu
A dried, sponge-like product made from wheat gluten. When rehydrated, it is soft and slightly chewy, absorbing the flavors of soups and broths. Find fu at Japanese or well-stocked Asian grocery stores, often labeled *yaki-fu* (baked fu) or *koya-fu* (freeze-dried fu). It's usually sold in small bags in the dried foods section. If you can't find it, small

cubes of dried tofu or even crouton-style puffed wheat can serve as a mild-textured substitute.

gyoza wrappers
Wheat-flour wrappers specifically made for gyoza dumplings, designed to crisp beautifully when pan-fried, steam well, and fold easily. Widely available in Asian supermarkets.

Japanese Worcestershire sauce
Often called chuno sauce, this thick brown tangy sauce is a popular condiment in Japan. The best-known brand is Bulldog, which is widely available in Asian and regular supermarkets.

kabocha squash
A Japanese winter squash with green skin and sweet, dense, orange flesh, similar to pumpkin or sweet potato. Widely available in Asian and regular supermarkets.

karashi mustard
Sold in tubes or in powder form at Japanese and Asian grocery stores. The powdered form is sometimes labeled "Oriental Hot Mustard."

kinako
A gold-colored powder made from roasted soybeans, widely used in Japanese sweets for its nutty, sweet flavor. Find it in Asian supermarkets or online.

kiriboshi daikon
These are daikon radish strips that have been dried and packaged. Sold at Japanese grocery stores.

komatsuna
A leafy green vegetable with a mild flavor that is becoming easier to find outside Japan. You may see it at farmers' markets or Asian grocery stores. It can be substituted with spinach or Swiss chard.

lotus root
The rhizome of the lotus plant, with holes running through, giving it that give an attractive, lacy appearance. You'll find it at most Asian grocery stores.

maitake mushrooms
Also known as "hen of the woods." A flavorful, earthy mushroom prized for its rich umami taste. Widely available at major grocery stores, Asian grocery stores and farmers' markets.

mirin
A sweet, alcoholic liquor made from rice. Although it is a beverage, nowadays it's used almost exclusively for cooking. It is so sweet that it's often used instead of sugar in various recipes, and is a staple in any Japanese kitchen. Mirin is available at Japanese grocery stores or online.

mitsuba
Sometimes sold as Japanese parsley or honeywort, this a mild and fresh-tasting herb used as a garnish. It is available at well-stocked Japanese grocery stores and general Asian stores. If you can't find it, substitute mizuna greens, flat leaf parsley or celery leaves.

myoga ginger buds
You may find these aromatic buds at Japanese grocery stores, or on online shopping sites, where they are sometimes spelled "mioga."

nagaimo yam
Sold fresh as long, pale, tuberous roots with slightly fuzzy skin. It is also sometimes sold vacuum-sealed. Sometimes labeled "Chinese yam," "mountain yam," or "long yam."

nori seaweed
Nori dried roasted seaweed is sold in packets of large or small sheets, available at regular supermarkets as well as at Japanese grocery stores.

Glossary of Ingredients

okara
Translated as "soybean pulp" or "tofu dregs." It's the fibrous, insoluble parts of the soybean after soy milk has been extracted. In Japan this is available very cheaply, but elsewhere it may be hard to find. If you have a tofu maker near you, ask them if they have okara—they may even give you some for free. If you make your own soy milk or tofu, you will have plenty of okara.

rice
For recipes in this book that call for rice, use medium-grain Japonica rice, sometimes labeled as "sushi rice" in the supermarket.

rice koji
Steamed rice that has been inoculated with koji fungus and Aspergillus oryzae (lactic acid bacteria), which enhances fermentation and flavor. You can find it sold fresh or dried at Japanese or Asian markets or online.

rice vinegar
Don't confuse rice vinegar with "sushi vinegar," which has added salt and sugar. You can find rice vinegar at regular supermarkets: try and find one made only with rice, without distilled alcohol added.

sake
For recipes in this book that call for sake, you can use regular drinking sake. You can also use cooking sake, which you can find in Asian markets.

sake lees
Sake lees are the creamy white solids left over after making sake. Sake lees comes in dried slabs, as a paste, or sometimes in powder form and can be bought at Japanese grocery stores or online.

sakura shrimp
These tiny dried shrimp are used as a flavoring ingredient. Find them at Japanese grocery stores.

sansho pepper
An aromatic, peppery spice with a citrusy tang and a tongue-numbing quality. Related to, but different from, Sichuan pepper. The peppercorns are dried and ground into a powder or pickled. The fresh young leaves, called *kinome*, are used as a garnish.

sesame oil
When sesame oil is called for in the recipes in this book, it is the dark, toasted sesame oil. Some recipes call for "light sesame oil" which is pale in color and made from raw sesame seeds.

sesame paste
Japanese sesame paste is made by grinding up roasted sesame seeds so it has a deeper flavor than tahini. Find it at Japanese or Asian grocery stores.

shichimi togarashi
A seven-spice mix that is a popular condiment in Japan. It is sometimes called *Nanami togarashi* or *nanairo*. Find it at Japanese or Asian grocery stores.

shimeji mushrooms
Also called "beech mushrooms." Small, clustered mushrooms with firm stems and nutty, umami-rich flavor. Widely available at major grocery stores, Asian grocery stores and farmers' markets.

shirasu-boshi
Tiny, boiled and semi-dried baby sardines used in Japanese dishes for a salty, umami-rich topping. Find them at Japanese or Korean grocery stores, usually in the refrigerated or frozen section.

92 The Miso Cookbook

shishito peppers
Green, mildly spicy, and sold fresh. Find them at Japanese grocery stores and farmers' markets.

shiso leaves
Green shiso leaves are widely used in Japanese cooking as a garnish, in salads and so on. They are light green, with spiky points. Find them at Japanese grocery stores. Shiso is fairly easy to grow from seed.

soybeans
Regular (yellow) soybeans have a mild flavor and firm texture when cooked.

soybeans, black
A darker variety, with a slightly sweeter, richer taste. Used in Japanese simmered dishes (*kuromame*), and valued for their high antioxidant content.

soybeans, green
Immature soybeans, often sold fresh or frozen as *edamame*, but also available dried. They are sweeter and nuttier in flavor than regular soybeans.

soy sauce
For the recipes in this book, use Japanese *koikuchi* soy sauce, a dark, all-purpose soy sauce with a balanced salty, savory flavor.

sudachi citrus
A small, tart Japanese citrus fruit with a sharp, aromatic flavor, often used as a seasoning in place of vinegar or lemon. Find at Japanese grocery stores. Substitute with lemon.

takana mustard greens
Sold pickled at Japanese grocery stores. A spicy, crunchy, umami-rich flavor.

taro root
Taro root is a starchy tuber with brown, hairy skin and white or purple-flecked flesh. It has a mildly sweet, nutty flavor and is often used in Japanese cuisine. Find at Asian grocery stores or farmers' markets.

tororo kombu
A type of shaved kelp made by slicing kelp (kombu) that's been softened with vinegar into ultra-thin, wispy strands. It has a soft, melting texture when added to hot liquid, giving a light, silky thickness and subtle umami. It's used in miso soup or poured over rice in Japanese home cooking. Find it at Japanese grocery stores, often near the dried seaweed or miso soup ingredients. It's typically sold in small plastic packets and may be labeled "shredded kelp." You can substitute with a little finely shredded wakame or a few pieces of reconstituted kombu.

turnip, Asian
Asian varieties, like the Japanese *kabu*, are small, round and white; they are sweeter and more tender than Western turnips. Find them at Asian grocery stores and farmers' markets.

white miso
Store-bought white miso can be used as a substitute for Homemade Miso in any of the recipes in this book. White miso is lightly fermented and has a mild, slightly sweet flavor. It has a lower salt content than red or brown miso.

udon noodles
These thick, chewy wheat noodles are available at Japanese grocery stores in either dried or fresh-frozen form.

umeboshi
Salt-preserved ume plums, related to apricots but much tarter when ripe. They are usually quite salty and sour, although some types are sweetened with honey or sugar. Umeboshi can be large and soft or small and hard; use the fleshier ones for the recipes in this book.

wakame seaweed
Has a sweet briny flavor and silky texture. It is sold dried at Asian grocery stores.

yuzu kosho
A spicy Japanese paste made from yuzu citrus and chili; available in small jars or tubes at Asian grocery stores.

Glossary of Ingredients 93

Index of Main Ingredients

adzuki beans
 Adzuki Bean Miso 14
asparagus
 Miso Soup with Asparagus and Onion 25
bacon
 Broccoli & Bacon Miso Gratin 50
 Miso Carbonara 55
 Tomato and Bacon Soup 28
banana
 Miso Banana Bread 80
beef
 Miso Bulgogi with Ginger 53
 Miso Hayashi Rice 56
bell pepper, green
 Green Pepper and Pork Miso Soup 25
bell pepper, red
 Miso Bulgogi with Ginger 53
bell pepper, yellow
 Korean-style Miso Bell Pepper Namul 68
bok choy
 Stir-fried Pork with Miso 42
bread
 Miso Butter Toast 34
broccoli
 Broccoli & Bacon Miso Gratin 50
burdock root
 Miso Kinpira 67
 Pork and Root Vegetable Miso Soup 21
cabbage
 Cabbage & Shrimp Miso Soup 24
 Chunky Vegetable Miso Stew 52
 Miso-flavored Gyoza Dumplings 49
cabbage, napa
 Cabbage and Pork Hot Pot with Miso 46
 Chicken & Cabbage Miso Soup 22
carrot
 Carrot with Walnuts 66
 Chunky Vegetable Miso Stew 52
 Daikon Stewed in Miso 69
 Miso Kinpira 67
 Onion and Carrot Miso Soup with Ginger 18
 Pork and Root Vegetable Miso Soup 21
cauliflower
 Miso Soup with Cauliflower 27
celery
 Chunky Vegetable Miso Stew 52

cheese
 cream
  Cheesy Miso Dip 72
  Miso Cheesecake 77
 Parmesan
  Miso Carbonara 55
 pizza
  Broccoli & Bacon Miso Gratin 50
 processed
  Chicken Spring Rolls with Miso 39
chicken
 Chicken & Cabbage Miso Soup 22
 Chicken Karaage with Miso 41
 Chicken with Lotus Root 66
 Chicken and Lotus Root Rice with Miso 60
 Chicken in Sesame Miso 45
 Chicken Spring Rolls with Miso 39
 Chilled Udon Noodles with Chicken 59
 Miso Butter Chicken Curry 57
 Miso Chicken Patties 43
chickpeas
 Chickpea Miso 14
chocolate, white
 Kinako Miso Truffles 75
chrysanthemum greens
 Greens with Miso and Tofu 67
corn kernels
 Potato and Corn Miso Soup with Soy Milk 29
cream, heavy
 Miso Cheesecake 77
 Miso Milk Pudding 78
cucumber
 Chilled Udon Noodles with Chicken 59
 Cucumber and Turnip Miso Pickles 65
 Cucumber with Vinegar Miso 68
daikon *see also* **kiriboshi**
 Pork and Root Vegetable Miso Soup 21
egg
 Fried Rice with Miso & Pickles 61
 Miso Carbonara 55
 Miso Cheesecake 77
 Miso Scrambled Eggs 36
 Miso Soup with Komatsuna and Egg 23
eggplant
 Eggplant Wrapped in Miso Pork 38
 Miso Soup with Eggplant 26

fu wheat gluten
 Wakame and Fu Instant Miso Soup 30
gochugaru chili powder
 Easy Gochujang Korean Chili Paste 86
gochujang chili paste
 Gochujang Miso Sauce 71
green beans
 Miso Butter Chicken Curry 57
gyoza wrappers
 Miso-flavored Gyoza Dumplings 49
honey
 Ma Lai Go Sponge Cake with Miso 79
hot dog
 Chunky Vegetable Miso Stew 52
ice cream
 Miso Ice Cream 74
kabocha squash
 Kabocha Miso Soup 28
kidney beans
 Chunky Vegetable Miso Stew 52
kimchi
 Spicy Miso Soup & Pea Shoots 23
kinako soybean powder
 Kinako Miso Truffles 75
kiriboshi daikon
 Daikon Stewed in Miso 69
komatsuna
 Miso Soup with Komatsuna and Egg 23
leek
 Cabbage and Pork Hot Pot with Miso 46
 Leek and Tofu Miso Soup 19
 Miso Sauce with Onion 71
lotus root
 Chicken with Lotus Root 66
 Chicken and Lotus Root Rice with Miso 60
mitsuba
 Mitsuba and Ginger Instant Miso Soup 32
mushrooms
 button
  Miso Hayashi Rice 56
 maitake
  Mushroom Miso Soup 26
 shimeji
  Mushroom Miso Soup 26

94   The Miso Cookbook

myoga ginger
    Miso Soup with Eggplant 26
    Myoga and Shiso Instant Miso Soup 32

nagaimo yam
    Miso Soup, Yam & Seaweed 22
    Yam and Okra Miso Soup 27

nam pla fish sauce
    Fish Sauce Koji 85

noodles
    Chinese
        Miso Soy Milk Tantanmen 58
    udon
        Chilled Udon Noodles with Chicken 59

okara soybean pulp
    Okara Miso 15

okra
    Yam and Okra Miso Soup 27

onion
    Miso Hayashi Rice 56
    Miso Soup with Asparagus and Onion 25
    Onion and Carrot Miso Soup with Ginger 18
    Onion Miso Dressing 70

peanuts
    Kinako Miso Truffles 75

pea shoots
    Spicy Miso Soup & Pea Shoots 23

pepper, shishito
    Grilled Salmon Marinated in Miso 64

pine nuts
    Fried Rice with Miso & Pickles 61

pork
    Cabbage and Pork Hot Pot with Miso 46
    Eggplant Wrapped in Miso Pork 38
    Green Pepper and Pork Miso Soup 25
    Miso-flavored Gyoza Dumplings 49
    Miso Soy Milk Tantanmen 58
    Pan-fried Pork Marinated in Miso 63
    Pork and Root Vegetable Miso Soup 21
    Stir-fried Pork with Miso 42

potato
    Miso Potatoes 69
    Potato and Corn Miso Soup with Soy Milk 29

rice
    Chicken and Lotus Root Rice with Miso 60
    Fried Rice with Miso & Pickles 61
    Miso Butter Chicken Curry 57
    Miso Hayashi Rice 56
    Miso Rice Balls with Shiso 35

rice koji
    Adzuki Bean Miso 14
    Amazake 87
    Black Soybean Miso 15
    Chickpea Miso 14
    Fish Sauce Koji 85
    Green Soybean Miso 14
    Homemade Miso 10
    Okara Miso 15
    Shio Koji 82
    Shoyu Koji 84
    Traditional Miso 88

sake lees
    Sake Lees Soup with Salmon and Taro 20

sakura shrimp
    Cabbage & Shrimp Miso Soup 24

salmon
    Grilled Salmon Marinated in Miso 64
    Sake Lees Soup with Salmon and Taro 20

sea bream
    Sea Bream with Miso & Butter 44

seaweed
    aosa
        Miso Soup, Yam & Seaweed 22
    nori
        Miso Butter Toast 34
        Nori and Sesame Instant Miso Soup 31
    tororo kombu
        Kombu and Umeboshi Instant Miso Soup 31
    wakame
        Wakame and Fu Instant Miso Soup 30

shirasu-boshi baby sardines
    Miso Soup with Turnip and Baby Sardines 24

shishito pepper
    Grilled Salmon Marinated in Miso 64

shiso leaf
    Chicken Spring Rolls with Miso 39
    Miso-flavored Gyoza Dumplings 49
    Miso Rice Balls with Shiso 35
    Myoga and Shiso Instant Miso Soup 32

soybeans
    black
        Black Soybean Miso 15
    green
        Green Soybean Miso 14
    regular
        Homemade Miso 10
        Traditional Miso 88

soy milk
    Chilled Udon Noodles with Chicken 59
    Ma Lai Go Sponge Cake with Miso 79
    Miso Sesame Cookies
    Miso Soy Milk Tantanmen 58
    Potato and Corn Miso Soup with Soy Milk 29

soy sauce
    Shoyu Koji 84

spaghetti
    Miso Carbonara 55

spinach
    Greens with Miso and Tofu 67

spring roll wrappers
    Chicken Spring Rolls with Miso 39

takana mustard greens
    Fried Rice with Miso & Pickles 61

taro root
    Sake Lees Soup with Salmon and Taro 20

tomato
    Miso Butter Chicken Curry 57
    Miso Hayashi Rice 56
    Sea Bream with Miso & Butter 44
    Tomato and Bacon Soup 28

tororo kombu *see* **seaweed**

tofu
    abura-age
        Daikon Stewed in Miso 69
    atsu-age
        Leek and Tofu Miso Soup 19
        Tofu with Miso Sauce 37
    silken
        Greens with Miso and Tofu 67

turnip
    Chicken in Sesame Miso
    Cucumber and Turnip Miso Pickles
    Miso Grilled Turnip
    Miso Soup with Turnip and Baby Sardines 24

umeboshi plum
    Chilled Udon Noodles with Chicken 59
    Kombu and Umeboshi Instant Miso Soup 31
    Umeboshi Miso Dressing 70

walnuts
    Walnut and Miso Dip 72

"Books to Span the East and West"

Tuttle Publishing was founded in 1832 in the small New England town of Rutland, Vermont [USA]. Our core values remain as strong today as they were then—to publish best-in-class books which bring people together one page at a time. In 1948, we established a publishing outpost in Japan—and Tuttle is now a leader in publishing English-language books about the arts, languages and cultures of Asia. The world has become a much smaller place today and Asia's economic and cultural influence has grown. Yet the need for meaningful dialogue and information about this diverse region has never been greater. Over the past seven decades, Tuttle has published thousands of books on subjects ranging from martial arts and paper crafts to language learning and literature—and our talented authors, illustrators, designers and photographers have won many prestigious awards. We welcome you to explore the wealth of information available on Asia at www.tuttlepublishing.com.

Published by Tuttle Publishing, an imprint of Periplus Editions (HK) Ltd.

www.tuttlepublishing.com

Karada ga Totonou "Hitoban Hakko Miso"
© 2021 Misa Enomoto
English translation rights arranged with
SHUFU-TO-SEIKATSU-SHA, CO., LTD.
through Japan UNI Agency, Inc., Tokyo

English translation by Makiko Itoh. English translation copyright ©2026 Periplus Editions (HK) Ltd.

All rights reserved. No part of this publication may be reproduced or utilized in any form or by any means, electronic or mechanical, including photocopying, recording, or by any information storage and retrieval system, without prior written permission from the publisher.

ISBN: 978-4-8053-1987-1

GPSR Representative
Matt Parsons, matt.parsons@upi2mbooks.hr
UPI-2M PLUS d.o.o., Medulićeva 20, 10000,
Zagreb, Croatia

Distributed by
North America, Latin America & Europe
Tuttle Publishing
364 Innovation Drive
North Clarendon, VT 05759-9436 U.S.A.
Tel: 1 (802) 773 8930 | Fax: 1 (802) 773 6993
info@tuttlepublishing.com
www.tuttlepublishing.com

Japan
Tuttle Publishing
Yaekari Building 3rd Floor
5-4-12 Osaki, Shinagawa-ku
Tokyo 141-0032
Tel: (81) 3 5437 0171 | Fax: (81) 3 5437 0755
sales@tuttle.co.jp | www.tuttle.co.jp

Asia Pacific
Berkeley Books Pte. Ltd.
3 Kallang Sector #04-01, Singapore 349278
Tel: (65) 6741 2178 | Fax: (65) 6741 2179
inquiries@periplus.com.sg
www.tuttlepublishing.com

28 27 26 25   6 5 4 3 2 1
Printed in China   2510EP

TUTTLE PUBLISHING® is a registered trademark of Tuttle Publishing, a division of Periplus Editions (HK) Ltd.